Late-Talking Children

Late-Talking Children

A Symptom or a Stage?

Stephen Camarata

The MIT Press
Cambridge, Massachusetts
London, England

MIT Press books may be purchased at special quantity discounts for business or sales promotional use. For information, please email special_sales@mitpress.mit.

This book was set in Stone Sans and Stone Serif by the MIT Press. Printed and bound in the United States of America.

Library of Congress Cataloging-in-Publication Data

Camarata, Stephen M., 1957- author.

Late-talking children : a symptom or a stage? / Stephen M. Camarata.

   pages   cm

Includes bibliographical references and index.

ISBN 978-0-262-02779-3 (hardcover : alk. paper)

1. Language disorders in children. 2. Language disorders in children—Diagnosis. 3. Children—Language. 4. Developmentally disabled children—Education. I. Title.

RJ496.L35C34 2014

618.92'855—dc23

2014003809

10 9 8 7 6 5 4 3 2

This book is dedicated to late-talking children and their families: May it help guide their journey!

Contents

Preface

The information in this book is a combination of personal experience, clinical observation, and scientific study. Long before I became a professor of hearing and speech, or a speech pathologist, I was already quite familiar with the anxiety experienced by parents of late-talking children. My own mother told me about the stress that she went through in the three years before I began to speak—a time when she was haunted by fears that I might never live a normal life. She was also plagued by the nagging question of whether she might have done something (or failed to do something) that caused me not to be able to speak.

My wife Mary Camarata (an accomplished speech language pathologist herself) and I also faced these haunting fears because one of our own children was also late talking. When he was just three years old, we were told that he would never go to college and that he belonged in a separate special education classroom for children with intellectual disabilities. Fortunately, those dire predictions did not come true. But I know firsthand what parents go through when their child doesn't begin talking on time.

This experience led me on a quest to understand why this dire, but incorrect, prediction was made and whether this was happening to other families with a late-talking child. Even at that time, more than 20 years ago, the available clinical and scientific literature should have prevented what happened to my son. Through this experience, I came to realize that parents themselves need information about late-talking children, so they can better navigate the confusing maze of diagnoses and treatment options.

In addition to being a late talker and the parent of a late-talking child, I have also been a speech pathologist for more than 30 years. I have tested and treated children whose late talking was a symptom of autism, apraxia, social communication disorder, speech and language disorders, as well as those with intellectual disability. Of course, I have also seen many whose late talking was simply a passing developmental stage rather than a symptom of a more serious condition. And I have seen those, like Albert Einstein, whose late talking was associated with high intelligence in mathematical or analytical ability. I have watched these children grow up and worked with them—and with their parents—through preschool, elementary, middle school, high school, and college. Along the way, I have learned about all the terrific services many of these children receive, but I have also seen the pitfalls, especially when a child is mislabeled, as was the case with my late-talking son.

I have also had the privilege of working with the many outstanding teachers and clinicians whose dedication and heroic efforts to teach and to treat late-talking children has been an inspiration. In an ideal world, all teachers and clinicians would be like these remarkable professionals so that parents could confidently seek answers for their late-talking child. Unfortunately, as was the case when my son was mislabeled as intellectually disabled, I have also had to help assist well-meaning, but misguided, teachers and clinicians understand that the labels they were using were not accurate and that treatments and educational programs derived from these labels were not beneficial. Sadly, far too many parents I have met in our clinical research program have reported that my experience with our late-talking son was not at all an isolated event and is instead an ongoing problem. These parents report encountering disbelief and condescension from some clinicians and teachers when asking reasonable questions about diagnosis, treatment, or educational programs for their own late-talking child.

As a scientist working in a highly ranked academic medical center, I have conducted dozens of studies with late-talking children of various types and have read hundreds of other studies on the subject. The gap between scientific knowledge on late-talking children and what is happening in the field is striking. Although there is still so very much that is not known, there is quite an extensive scientific literature to guide clinicians as they diagnose and treat late-talking children. Unfortunately, parents may encounter clinicians who are not current in their knowledge and implementation of this scientific literature. In fact, some clinicians may not even be aware of the well-established finding that most late-talking children do not have autism, apraxia, intellectual disability, or any other dire condition so that they mistakenly try to diagnose all late-talking children with one or more of these conditions.

Several years ago, I met with one of the world's leading pediatricians, who, at the time was director of a major children's hospital in Los Angeles. As we were discussing the problems facing parents seeking information on late-talking children when there are so many misconceptions—and outright deceptive practices— they may encounter. His sage advice was to write a book providing parents with accurate, up-to-date information, so they can be in a position to demand accurate diagnosis and proper treatment for their late-talking child. Acting on this advice, I wrote this book so that parents—and interested clinicians and other professionals—can learn the facts and fallacies related to late-talking children and realize that often it is a developmental stage that some children go through rather than a symptom of a serious disability. I've also included a set of action steps that parents can take when they need to develop the right diagnosis, treatment, and education plans their child will need if the late talking is a symptom of autism, speech disorders, social communication disorder, intellectual disability or another medical condition. And, these action steps also include methods for correcting labels and treatments that may be pushed upon them by well-meaning, but misguided experts who have inadequate information about late-talking children and misunderstandings about the particular child being evaluated.

As I say in the chapters ahead, another key is remembering that talking late is often a harbinger of your child's learning style: other things may come late too. So don't panic if your child is a late talker. Instead, learn everything you can about late-talking children and how to advocate effectively for your child. Even if the late talking is a symptom of autism or some other long-lasting condition, there are steps that parents can take to improve their child's future. We'll begin this crucial learning process in the pages that follow.

Acknowledgments

I am indebted to many people who have directly or indirectly supported the development of this book. First and foremost is my own late-talking son, who inadvertently set my feet on the path to writing a book for parents and clinicians because of our own experiences, good and bad, as we sought help for him. The inspiration and support of my wife Mary has also been crucial in so many ways. I learned through her eyes about the unique hopes and fears so many mothers have as they raise a late-talking child. Because I also talked late, she helped me understand what my own mother must have gone through, first in the years before I started talking and then later as there were "rough spots" when I went to schools that were not conducive to adjusting the curriculum to the learning styles that work best with late-talking children. Mary also talked me out of including a chapter entitled "Late Talkers: You Married One and You Have One," reflecting on the difficulties that she and many other spouses and parents encounter when living with a partner and a child who display the strong-willed tendencies seen in many late-talking children. She has unfailingly been a terrific mother and advocate for our late-talking son, while patiently tolerating my own "late-talker" idiosyncrasies.

I also wish to thank those many dedicated families who have visited our clinical research program over the years. They get up every day and help their own late-talking child, regardless of whether it is a symptom or a stage for their child, in a world that does not always understand and support raising and educating a late-talking child. Some of these parents have formed a parent-moderated listserve that allows parents to connect with one another at latetalkkids@yahoogroups.com.

In addition, helpful information can be found on the website for the Late Talking Children's Foundation at latetalkers.org. A portion of the royalties from this book will be donated to support this foundation. The research in this book has been supported by the generous contributions of the Scottish Rite Foundation of Nashville, the Wallace Foundation, and from research grants from the US Department of Education and the US Institute for Educational Sciences. Research grants from the National Institutes of Health, including the National Institute on Child Health and Human Development, the National Institute of Mental Health, and the National Institute on Deafness and Other Communication Disorders also supported these studies.

I am also indebted to the clinicians and scientists who have been guiding lights in my intellectual life. Sandy Fey and Jeanette Leonard were two of the many outstanding clinicians whose example was crucial as I learned about assessment and treatment of children with speech and language disorders. Professors Robert and Lynn Koegel at the Koegel Autism Center are also two of the most dedicated scientists and clinicians I know. Their tireless work has helped thousands of families whose late-talking child has autism. Their books *Pivotal Response Training* and *Overcoming Autism* are beacons of hope for those serving people with autism. In addition, Professor Laurence Leonard at

Purdue University is without a doubt the world's leading expert on language disorders in children. His book *Specific Language Impairment* provides a thorough review of the current knowledge on this condition. I was blessed to have had the benefit of his wisdom, guidance, and support during the early stages of my own development as a clinical scientist and his ongoing friendship since then.

In addition, Dr. Bill Long, a pediatrician, and Kristina Farr, a parent of a late-talking child provided helpful comments on an earlier draft of the manuscript. My daughter-in-law, Ryan Camarata, also read the manuscript and provided helpful suggestions. The folks at MIT Press are owed thanks as well. My editor Philip Laughlin has been supportive, professional, and helpful throughout. Marcy Ross deserves high praise for her diligence and patience as the production editor of the manuscript, and Elizabeth Judd copyedited the manuscript with great care and offered valuable suggestions.

Finally, deepest thanks are extended to Professors Thomas Sowell of the Hoover Institution at Stanford University and Steven Pinker at Harvard University. Dr. Sowell has been unwavering in his support of this project and is both a dear friend and mentor. His editorial column describing his own late-talking son and his excellent books on late-talking children (*Late-Talking Children* and *The Einstein Syndrome*) were the catalysts for our ongoing interactions about late-talking children. Dr. Pinker is not only a world-renowned cognitive scientist and author (his books *The Language Instinct* and *Words and Rules* are especially relevant for language development), he is a very kind and caring person who generously has given his time and expertise to facilitate the development of this book.

1 A Symptom or a Stage?

Children are late in beginning to talk for all sorts of reasons, so there is no one-size-fits-all explanation or any one-size-fits-all treatment. The mental level of late-talking children ranges from severely intellectually disabled (the condition that used to be referred to as "mentally retarded") all the way up to, and including, Albert Einstein, who was three years old before he talked. In my 31 years of treating late-talking children, I have encountered late-talking children who were brilliant; children with intellectual disabilities, severe autism, or other medical problems; and many who were simply normal except for being slow to begin speaking.

Late talking may be a stage that some children pass through, while for others their delayed speech may be a symptom of much bigger problems, including some that will be with them for life. This means that parents of late-talking children have a lot of anxiety and stress to cope with, while waiting to hear that first word or phrase.

Parental Anxiety

Not only have I seen many distressed parents—some in tears—in my clinical research program at the Vanderbilt University

Medical School; I knew about the stress that such parents can go through long before I became a professor of hearing and speech. While I was growing up, my own mother told me about the stress that she went through during the three years before I began to speak—the haunting fears that I might never live a normal life, and the nagging question of whether it might have been something that she did, or didn't do, that caused me not to be able to speak.

My wife and I also know these haunting fears because one of our own children was late talking as well. When he was three years old, we were told that he would never go to college and that he belonged in a separate special-education classroom for children with intellectual disabilities (which was then called mental retardation). As will be seen later in this book, these dire predictions thankfully did not come true. Because of this, I do know firsthand what parents go through when their precious child does not begin talking on time.

These are natural concerns for parents when years go by without a child saying anything, or perhaps saying no more than a few isolated words, while other children of the same age are speaking in sentences or even engaging in back-and-forth conversations. However, despite having seen many guilt-ridden parents over the years, I have found that the late talking is almost never due to anything the parents have done or not done, even though too many people, including some clinicians, have been too quick to blame parents—especially mothers.

Although practical problems can arise when a child is unable to communicate, my experience with the hundreds and hundreds of patients I have seen over the years has been that these problems are seldom the main reason for parental anxiety. The same conclusion is shown by the data on an informal group of more than six hundred families with late-talking children whose parents are in touch with us, and with each other, by email, phone, or postal mail across the United States and in a number of foreign countries, including England, China, Brazil, Australia, and Saudi Arabia.

The primary reason that 64 percent of the parents in this large group gave for being concerned about their children was that the child was behind schedule in developing the ability to speak. Another 12 percent were concerned because their child seemed frustrated in not being able to communicate. Only 9 percent cited practical problems created by the lack of verbal communication.

Although late-talking children often find other ways of communicating what they want, whether by pointing, by leading their parent by the hand, or through some other means, parents are nevertheless worried about the child's delay in beginning to speak—and there are good reasons to be concerned, given some of the possibilities, even if most of these late-talking children end up with no long-term problems as they grow up. Parents can never know whether there will be permanent problems when the child is still at the stage of saying nothing.

There is no point playing Russian roulette, even if the gun goes off only about one-sixth of the time. Getting a reliable evaluation is very important in not letting concern become panic. No one should assume their child will "grow out of" the late talking, even though many late-talking children do just that.

Among the many families in our informal international group, 608 have filled out questionnaires for their children. Of these children, 439 have received some kind of evaluation. Because they are so widely scattered, most of these evaluations have been done by others elsewhere, rather than in our clinical research program. The most common conclusion from these evaluations has been that there is simply a speech/language delay (25 percent). Other conclusions range from hearing problems (3 percent) to a more general delay in development (12 percent), rather than a delay in speech development alone. For 13 percent of these late-talking children, no reason could be determined as to why they were not yet speaking, and for 9 percent the diagnosis was autism.

Because I have not evaluated most of these children myself, there is no way of knowing which of these diagnoses were well founded, much less which will turn out to be valid as the years go by, though the 9 percent rate of autism among late-talking children is consistent with information from other sources. The point in mentioning these data at all is simply to illustrate that there are a variety of possible reasons why children might talk late.

Because there are so many very different reasons why a particular child is not talking at an age when most other children have begun to speak, getting a reliable professional diagnosis is very important. But finding a reliable professional diagnosis is not always easy because, frankly, there are too many well-meaning but misguided people who are far too willing to put a label on a child, based on a checklist of "symptoms" of autism or intellectual disabilities or some other dire condition without considering alternatives. It is all too easy to start off with a preconceived notion and then find evidence that seems to confirm this preordained diagnosis using a checklist. But that is *not* a proper medical or scientific method of diagnosis.

What makes checklists unreliable and dangerous when used improperly is that many children pass through a stage when they have some of the same characteristics that are taken as symptoms of lifelong conditions such as autism, even when these children are neither autistic nor afflicted with any other lasting disabilities. Checklists are no substitute for the professional training and experience required to separate out children for whom late talking is just a passing phase from other children for whom the late talking is a symptom of deeper and more long-lasting problems.

As someone trained to test for autism symptoms, and who has served on scientific committees of the National Institutes of Health that reviews research on autism and other disabilities, I know that a checklist *by itself* is often too unreliable for making decisions that can change a child's life fundamentally, for better or worse. When there are a number of sources of information, a checklist may be useful as one of those sources, despite being dangerous as a sole or decisive source. It is not surprising that many studies have shown that checklists are accurate *only* when used in conjunction with sound clinical judgment.[1]

In my own clinical work, I have encountered numerous children who have been falsely diagnosed as having autism, intellectual disabilities, or other dire conditions. Often these mistaken diagnoses are made by people not properly trained to recognize the symptoms of more dire conditions as distinct from simply talking late. This may include well-meaning but misguided teachers, speech pathologists, nurses, occupational therapists, and in some cases even physicians, or it can just be neighbors or family members who have read some newspaper or magazine article or come across some checklist on the Internet or elsewhere. Not only have many parents been devastated by false diagnoses, too many children have been subjected to treatments for autism or intellectual disabilities or other severe conditions that can be both traumatic and counterproductive for those who do not have these conditions.

While early intervention can indeed be very helpful to some children, it can be harmful to others. The treatment has to be appropriate for the condition. Radiation treatment is needed when a patient has some kinds of cancer, but no one would use such a treatment when the patient doesn't have cancer.

Many painful examples come to mind from my experiences over the years. A late-talking little boy from Nebraska was an example of how the wrong early intervention can do harm. He was diagnosed by a school psychologist as having both autism and intellectual disabilities and was put in a preschool class for children with severe disabilities.

Tests given to him during the two years he was in that class showed that he made no real progress in all that time. The parents then changed their minds about accepting the class placement and turned to me for a second opinion. My examination of him led me to conclude that he should not be in that class. Everyone agreed that he was behind in talking and needed early intervention, but I disagreed that the special class was the right kind of intervention.

I had to fly to Nebraska for a special hearing on the child's education, in order to get him transferred to a regular class. The school district wanted to keep him in a segregated class for children with severe autism, but we were able to get him transferred into a regular second-grade classroom. When he entered that class, tests showed that his educational progress was lagging years behind that of the children who had been in a regular class all along. However, in less than two years, new tests showed that he had caught up with his classmates in many ways. His mother reported that he "blossomed" in the second grade, and subsequent testing bears this out. He still needed special help to learn, but it was clear that the regular class was a much better early intervention.

In short, the two years of the wrong kind of early intervention clearly had held back his progress, but getting the right intervention resulted in dramatic progress. Not all children may be that fortunate, especially if the incorrect early intervention is prolonged. This clinical impression was confirmed by a scientific review of early intervention that appeared in the prestigious medical journal *Pediatrics*. The authors reviewed the literature on early intervention and concluded: "The strength of the evidence overall [to support early intervention] ranged from insufficient to low."[2] How can this possibly be? After all, everyone *"knows"* that early intervention works. But *"knowing"* and *"proving"* are not the same thing.

An example from medicine illustrates this point. Meningitis is a serious illness arising from inflammation of the membrane surrounding the brain and spinal cord. Bacterial meningitis is particularly dangerous and can result in death, permanent cognitive impairment, seizures, and/or hearing loss. Early intervention is crucial for reducing the risk of these complications. The primary symptoms are fever and headache. Fortunately, meningitis can be diagnosed using a medical test that can detect the bacteria causing the illness. But, imagine what would happen if all patients with a headache and a fever were placed on a "meningitis spectrum." Attempts to test the effectiveness of early intervention would be confounded by this overly broad definition. Taking aspirin, or even doing nothing would have a high "cure" rate for the "meningitis spectrum," but would do nothing for the patients on the more severe end of this "spectrum" who actually have meningitis. One can not help but wonder whether this is happening with the expansion of the autism spectrum.

Another late-talking little boy was brought to me from New York because he had been diagnosed as having autism. My testing showed that was not true, but the people who had diagnosed him back in New York could not be convinced. When the boy began to walk on his toes and to bite his hand, they felt this was proof they were right, because toe walking and self-injuring are things many children with autism do.

When his mother informed me of what he was doing, I immediately suggested that she take him to a specialist in self-injuries

and to a neurologist. Perfectly normal people sometimes deliberately cause themselves pain, such as by biting their lip, to mask
some other pain they are feeling. Moreover, problems in the
brain other than autism can cause both pain and toe walking.

The neurologist discovered that this little boy had a brain
tumor, and he was operated on to remove it. The neurologist
told his mother that her son could have died within a year if
the tumor had not been discovered. One of the many problems
with false diagnoses is that those who have made such diagnoses can become wedded to their conclusions, and subsequently
interpret whatever the child does within the framework of their
diagnosis, ignoring other possibilities that need to be considered
and tested. This little boy needed early intervention—for a brain
tumor—but the incorrect diagnosis he had received for autism
was the biggest obstacle to his being tested for other possibilities.

After children have a label like intellectual disabilities or autism
put on them, parents as well as others who deal with them can
come to view them differently, and to behave toward them differently than they would toward other children. Not only does that
disrupt the natural development of the early parent-child rela-
tionship, it makes many parents more willing to hand their children over to strangers who claim to know what's best, but who
can't have the same devotion parents have to their own child.

When children are late in beginning to speak, many people
begin to scrutinize their every action, seeing "symptoms" and
"red flags" of something wrong in things that might otherwise
be seen as typical of the odd things toddlers often do, which are
regarded as cute when the child is *not* a late talker.

As an example, one little preschooler that I was treating for
his speech delay liked to pick fuzz off a carpet and play with it.
A psychologist said that this was one of the signs of autism. I
then showed him a videotape of 13 children in that toddler's

preschool class, 6 of whom were picking fuzz off the carpet and playing with it. But none of the other 5 children were regarded as having a symptom of autism, because they were talking.

Improper labeling of late-talking children is one of the dangers parents have to be on guard against.

Diagnosis and Treatment

Early *diagnosis* of late-talking children and early intervention by a qualified professional are both very important, even though the wrong kind of early intervention can do lasting damage if the diagnosis is not accurate. In short, early intervention can be either a blessing or a curse, depending on the reliability of the diagnosis, the specific intervention, and the particular child. There is another serious question to consider: When is an early diagnosis *too* early? I have had parents come to me with children as young as 12 months old, because their toddlers were not yet talking, and some checklists say that they should begin speaking by the time they are a year old.

While it is true that most small children say at least a word by the time they are a year old, there is a perfectly normal variation from child to child. It is not easy to diagnose a late-talking child before the age of 18 months, unless there is a severe disorder that can be clearly and reliably diagnosed earlier, such as Down syndrome, cerebral palsy, or severe autism.[3] I am very cautious when diagnosing toddlers because not only is a variation in the age of speaking common, there are serious difficulties in trying to accurately diagnose a very young child for some things for which late talking is a symptom—and an inaccurate diagnosis can be too harmful to risk.

It is understandable that parents want to know what is happening, as early as possible, both for the sake of the child and for their own peace of mind. But there is no point in giving them a diagnosis that I cannot have confidence in myself.

None of this means that parents of late-talking children should not worry. Worry goes with the territory of being a parent—and that is a child's much-needed protection. Autism is just one of the devastating things for which late talking may be a symptom. From time to time, I have had the painful duty of having to tell parents that their child has autism, intellectual disabilities, or some other dire affliction. Knowing how hard that is on me, I can only imagine how much harder it must be for the parents. But you need to know things like that sooner rather than later— but only *if* an accurate diagnosis can be made.

When Should a Child Be Considered Late in Beginning to Speak?

Some rough guidelines can be useful, provided you do not take them as ironclad rules indicating something terrible is happening if the child is a few weeks or a couple of months behind schedule. Children do not all develop in lockstep.

Because talking usually develops in stages, we need to define those stages carefully before we can say that a particular child is significantly late in developing the ability to speak. The first stage is simply using a word, whether for a person or a thing. Just making a sound is not using a word, even if it is a sound used to designate something. For example, when a child points to a toy or some food that he or she wants and says "ha," that is not really a word, even though it shows that the child sees a connection between making a particular sound and trying to indicate a particular thing.

It is when a child uses a *recognizable* word to designate a person or a thing that we can say that this first stage of speech development has been reached. For most children this happens some time between 9 and 18 months, though there is no need to panic if it takes a little longer and the child is otherwise developing fine.

Often the child will add to the number of isolated words in his or her vocabulary as time goes on, before reaching the next stage, which is using more than one word in combination with others. It may be just a short phrase, like "go bye-bye," rather than a complete sentence. But that still represents an advance. This stage is usually reached by two years of age, when the "average" number of spoken words is about 100. But even in "typical" development, the range is anywhere from 20 to over 180 words for a two year old.[4]

Then, as the child grows older, the phrases tend to grow longer. One rough rule is that the number of words in a phrase is about one-tenth the number of months that the child is old. For example, a child who is 30 months old might be expected to use three words together and a child who is 40 months old might be expected to use four words together.

Again, *these are just rough guidelines*, rather than reasons to panic if your child doesn't conform strictly to this pattern. But at least these guidelines allow us to say that a child is or is not a late talker.

When it is clear that your child is significantly late in developing the ability to speak, it is time to get a medical evaluation from a pediatrician or some other qualified health professional to ensure there are no medical problems causing the late talking (such as a brain tumor or seizures). After the medical exam has been completed, then an evaluation with a speech pathologist, psychologist, or special educator may be recommended.

However, parents seeking a diagnosis of their late-talking child need to know at the outset that a reliable diagnosis may not be easy to find. Multiple diagnoses from sources indepen-dent of each other are often advisable.

Quite frankly, unsubstantiated beliefs, fads, fashions, dogmas, and scams can flourish in a situation where desperate parents are putting their trust in "experts" who have few checks or balances, as far as the accuracy of the diagnoses they make or the actual effects of the treatments they prescribe are concerned. There are also financial incentives to put labels on children that will enable their treatment to be paid for by government programs or by health insurance, whether or not those labels accurately reflect the child's actual situation. In my experience, the over-whelming majority of clinicians working with late-talking chil-dren are well meaning and honest.

Moreover, even honest people who are trying to do their best to help a late-talking child can go wrong in a field where there are inadequate rigorous institutional standards requiring empiri-cal evidence to back up beliefs or fashions about diagnoses or treatments.

Common Fallacies

Many treatments are believed to be effective because children not talking before end up talking after those treatments. And this is offered as evidence that a treatment "works." But I have seen the fallacy in this from my own experience.

Some years ago, a colleague at Vanderbilt University brought her daughter to me for treatment because the little girl was not talking. I did not think treatment was called for yet, for a child who was only 16 months old and who showed no other prob-lems. But I told the mother I would videotape her daughter every month, so that we could follow her progress. After a few months, the little girl began to talk and her mother, who was greatly relieved, expressed her gratitude for my treatment. But I gave her daughter *no* treatment. All I did was videotape. "You may as well thank Panasonic," I said, "since they made the video camera— and all I did was operate the camera."

When I happened to encounter the same mother and daughter at a store years later, the daughter was talking away on her cellphone, and the mother found it ironic that she had once been worried about the girl's not talking.

This girl was not unique. Many late-talking children eventually begin talking on their own.[5] Internationally recognized language authority and neuroscientist Professor Steven Pinker of Harvard says that "language seems to develop about as quickly as the growing brain can handle it."[6] What that means is that *any* treatment—no matter how ineffective—used before the child's natural brain development leads to the ability to speak can look "effective" because the child spoke after a treatment was applied—just as he or she would have if *no* treatment had been provided. It is simply coincidence the child began speaking after the "treatment" was provided.

Because of this, some people are convinced that taking a heavy dose of vitamins, wearing a weighted vest, or some other questionable treatment is what enabled their late-talking child to finally begin to speak.

Here again, both logic and my own professional experience show the fallacy in such reasoning. Because our clinical research program usually has more children whose parents are seeking treatment than we can begin treating immediately, there is a waiting list. In quite a number of cases, late-talking children on that waiting list began to speak before we had a chance to give them any treatment at all.

If, as Professor Pinker suggested, talking tends to begin whenever a young child's growing brain reaches a certain level of development, that could also help explain why so many earnest efforts, by parents and professionals alike, may produce no results at all, even when they are doing things that are effective with other children. When the time is right—in terms of that particular child's own brain development—he or she may begin to speak spontaneously. This sometimes happens after frustrated parents and professionals have already given up hope and stopped doing anything: The child's brain was simply not yet ready, no matter what was tried.

It would be wrong to automatically attribute children's speaking to whatever treatment may have been used, when the same outcome can occur after such things as just videotaping them or putting them on a waiting list. But this kind of fallacy is very understandable in human terms. It goes back centuries, when it was called the *post hoc, ergo propter hoc* fallacy—that is, the belief that because one thing happens after another, the first thing is what caused the second.[7] Just because it is something human beings have done for centuries, that does not make it any less of a fallacy.

Sometimes there is a strong emotional reason to commit this fallacy. In one case, a pediatrician in Pennsylvania was getting ready to inoculate a little girl with a vaccine when she suddenly went into violent seizures. Had that pediatrician been working just a little faster, he would have injected that vaccine first. In that case, imagine if the mother had been looking on as her apparently perfectly healthy daughter was injected and then suddenly went into seizures. It would certainly have been understandable—from an emotional standpoint—if that mother was convinced the vaccine caused her daughter's seizures. Only the accident of timing prevented that particular fallacy in this case.

Incidentally, all parts of a child's brain do not necessarily develop in lockstep, any more than all children develop in lockstep, so a late-talking child's general intelligence may be normal or even noticeably above normal, when that child's ability to speak is either below normal or nonexistent. We have had a child in our clinical research program who was not saying one word, but whose IQ on a nonverbal test was over 140, compared to a national average of 100 for children his age.

Treatment and Mistreatment

Systematic, scientific procedures have been developed that can be used to test whether a particular treatment is really the reason for a late-talking child's beginning to speak. Such procedures are commonly used in medical science to test whether particular pharmaceutical drugs or particular medical treatments are in fact effective.[8] But there is no professional institution to *compel* the use of scientific testing procedures before a particular treatment for late-talking children is accepted as valid. That is why so many questionable procedures continue to be used to treat speech and language delays, despite an absence of any scientific evidence to validate the effect of those treatments.

Even in cases where scientific procedures have shown a particular treatment to be no more effective than a placebo, that ineffective treatment can continue to be widely used, when there is no professional organization or government agency with both the will and the power to ban such procedures. It is an open invitation to quackery. Sometimes it is worse than quackery; it is child abuse.

Pressure, and even force, is sometimes used, in order to try to *make* a child talk. Some children have been strapped into a chair, where they are confronted with the clinician's demands to say words. Many children become upset and traumatized at being tied to a chair and start crying. Sometimes the mother cries too, but because parents are told this is necessary to help their child, many parents go along with this "treatment." Children sometimes become less social, and some even stop whatever talking they had been doing before, after such traumatic "treatment."

In later years, some children tied to chairs have reported their lasting anger about that experience. If a particular child's brain has not yet developed to the point where talking is possible, such draconian methods are as futile as they are cruel.

Such treatment—or mistreatment—has especially been used when a child has been labeled "autistic," whether or not that diagnosis actually applies. I have had some clinicians tell me that you have to "break" a child with autism the way you break a horse. The child is helpless in the hands of such zealots but the parents are not—and should not go along with things that their own common sense tells them are wrong, even if a clinician condescendingly tells them that they are "in denial" if they don't. Parents should *always* be viewed as partners in the treatment process, not as obstacles to be overcome.

Think about it: to encourage talking, children should learn that parents and other adults are positive and nurturing. But what happens when adults seize the children and restrain them in chairs? What are those children learning about being social with adults? Sadly, even parents whose common sense tells them that their children should not be treated this way end up going along because they have been told this is "necessary" to teach a child how to talk. Of course, this is not true and is not supported in the scientific literature.

I personally have helped hundreds and hundreds of children learn to talk and have *never* strapped any of them into these kinds of chairs or restrained a child like this. I can say with 100 percent certainty that restraint and force are not *required* to teach a child how to talk. I can point to more than 100 studies showing the benefits of speech and language treatment without resorting to restraint. It is now up to the proponents of restraint as a means of teaching children to speak to conduct unbiased *scientific* studies proving that approach provides any additional benefit or does not cause harm. In the absence of such studies, do not allow anyone to strap your child into a chair or otherwise restrain the child in the name of "treatment" for their late talking.

The stakes are just too high to let children be subjected to needless stress and danger, without at least getting second or third opinions. Don't let anyone tell you that the wrong kind of early intervention can't hurt! I have seen too many children it has in fact hurt.

While parents of late-talking children will have to deal with many uncertainties and pitfalls, there are also ways of dealing with these challenges, many of which are discussed in later chapters. However, parents must first be equipped with knowledge about what is known or not known about why some children begin to speak years later than others. This is the subject of the next chapter.

2   What Do We Know about Late-Talking Children?

Although no one knows all the answers as to why some children begin talking much later—sometimes years later—than others, we do know some things about different patterns for different children. More important, we also know what kinds of treatments have been effective in some kinds of situations, as well as what rare kinds of situations defy all efforts to develop a child's ability to speak.

The most striking aspect in studies of late-talking children is that many catch up after a few years. As Dr. Laurence Leonard, a leading scholar, reported in the May 2009 issue of the *American Journal of Speech-Language Psychology*, "Slow expressive language development is not a good predictor of later language impairment." He cited studies in which most children with "specific language impairment"—one form of late talking, but with no other known disability—were no longer impaired in their speech at the age of five. In one study, just under 9 percent of these children were still impaired in their speech when they were five years old, and in another study under 8 percent were.[1] In plain English, this means that there were no significant long-term problems in most of the children who talk late in these studies!

And this is by no means an isolated finding. Professor Philip Dale, a scientist who studies language development and coauthor

of the book *Late Talkers* summarizes the scholarly research on
late-talking children by noting: "On the one hand, late talking is
demonstrably a risk condition for below average language development throughout childhood and into adolescence" [thus, a
symptom]. ... "On the other hand, it is also well established by
now that many children with language delays at age 2 or 3 will
score in the normal range 2 or 3 years later" [thus, a stage].[2] This
favorable outcome has been seen over and over again in studies of late-talking children not only in the United States, but in
other countries as well. For example, a study of late-talking children in Victoria, Australia, showed that more than 60 percent
who were not speaking at age two had "resolved" (caught up)
by the time they were four years old.[3] The British psychologist
Dorothy Bishop and her colleagues, including Dr. Dale, studied
another group of two-year-old late-talking children in England.
They reported, "At three years, [only] 44.1 percent of the ELD
[expressive language delay] group ... met criteria for persistent
language delay, decreasing slightly to 40.2% at 4 years ... consistent with previous reports of *frequent spontaneous resolution* of
delayed language in preschoolers."[4] Once again, the "spontaneous resolution" rate was about 60 percent.

Studies of late-talking children have also been conducted
in the United States, with the same results: 60 percent, or
more, catch up after a few years, or even faster. Professor Grover Whitehurst, who later became the first director of the
Institute for Educational Sciences at the U.S. Department of
Education, published a number of studies tracing the development of late-talking children. In one of the early studies
on the development of two-year-old late-talking children that
appeared in the journal *Pediatrics* in 1989[5], he found that after
only five months, one-third of the children had made significant improvement, essentially recovering fully. Another

one-third made moderate improvement, not yet catching up, but making steady progress on their speech development while only one-third essentially made no progress.

In another study conducted in the United States, Professor Leslie Rescorla from Bryn Mawr College in Pennsylvania followed a group of late-talking children from the age of 2 until age 17, when they were in high school. She also followed a matched set of children who did not talk late. At the end of this study, when the late-talking children were 17 years old, language ability was classified using quotients, wherein a "normal" score is anywhere between 85 and 115, with an average of 100 (like IQ tests). Of course, at the start of the study, all of the late-talking children were far behind on the measures of speaking ability, with an estimated expressive language quotient of about 75. But, at age 17, the authors reported that "the late talkers generally obtained scores in the average range or above on the language and reading/writing measures administered."[6] By then, the average expressive language quotient in the late-talking group was approximately 103 and the reading quotient was 104. In plain English, most were talking and reading just fine by the time they were young adults.

But, Dr. Rescorla emphasized that even though the overwhelming majority of late-talking children eventually caught up with their peers who did not talk late, as a group, the late-talking children are not quite as good on tasks that rely on speaking and listening. It was clear that late-talking children perform better on nonverbal thinking skills than they do on verbal tasks: "Although late talkers continued to be comparable with SES [socioeconomic status] matched comparison children on nonverbal tasks [such as math computation and nonverbal reasoning], their scores on most of the age 17 language measures were lower than those of the comparison children, despite being in the average range."[7] In short, in much the same way a clumsy young child may not excel at athletics later on (although some do), late-talking children tend not to excel at speaking and listening as they grow up. This relative weakness has profound implications for how to best teach late-talking children, a topic that will be dealt with in chapter 9.

The fact that most late-talking children recover on their own also has important implications for studying the effect of early intervention. As long as any "treatment" does no harm, 60 percent (or more) of the children enrolled in "early intervention" will catch up in a year or two, even when the "treatment" doesn't provide any benefit whatsoever! One-third will likely demonstrate rapid growth after only five months. Imagine if these children were misidentified as having "autism spectrum disorder" at age two and then given worthless treatment. Parents and clinicians may be fooled into thinking they had somehow "cured" the autism by the child's fourth birthday or even sooner.

Predicting Which Late-Talking Children Will Catch Up

The scientific literature on late-talking children also provides important clues for predicting who will catch up (a stage), and who will not (a symptom). For example, some late-talking children clearly understand what is being said to them and can follow directions to do particular things. It is not uncommon for some of these children to be more advanced in their understanding, and in their ability to follow directions, than other children their age who are talking. There is a very different situation, however, when a child neither speaks nor shows any understanding of what is being said.[8] When these two very different kinds of late-talking children have been followed over time, the former have usually turned out much better than the latter. Indeed, they have often developed quite normally after they have gotten past the initial late-talking stage, and some have turned out to have significantly higher than average intelligence.

Another study also found that when 24-month-old children have difficulties understanding words as well as using words, "their outcomes are poorer."[9] While this is a cause for serious concern, it is not inevitably written in stone that every child who neither speaks nor understands what is said will end up with life-long challenges.

Yet another study showed that a late-talking child's level of comprehension at three years of age was the strongest single predictor of these children's language scores at age five: "Language comprehension at 3 years was the best predictor of later language and early reading."[10] That is, even if children aren't talking at 30 months, how well they understand what others are saying is a good predictor of how well they'll be talking by the age of five and a half.

In addition to how much a child understands, other factors that predict who will catch up, and who will not, include how much a child vocalizes, how many different kinds of sounds are made prior to using words, whether there is pretend play, whether the child tries to communicate using gestures or other nonverbal strategies, and whether they imitate the actions of parents or others. The more a late-talking child does any of these things, the more likely they are to catch up. Stated simply, when a late-talking child understands what is said to them, engages in pretend play, vocalizes frequently using a variety of sounds (such as "ba," "ga," "da," and "ma"), enjoys playing with and being around other people, tries to imitate what other people do, and attempts to communicate using gestures, they are more likely to catch up.[11] But, no parent should look at the traits that predict spontaneous recovery and decide that their child "fits" the profile of those who recover.

The fact that the vast majority of late-talking children have no long-term problems, of course, is no reason for complacency. I worry that anyone reading this book would automatically assume that their own late-talking child is one of the 60 percent—or more—that will eventually catch up. Even if the chances are six out of ten that the late talking is a passing stage with no long-term problems, some of the things that can happen if the late talking is a symptom rather than a passing phase are sufficiently dire to guard against. Parents should seek one or more *independent* diagnoses by a highly qualified person or persons, at least one of whom should be a physician. *All* late-taking children should have a thorough medical examination and also be tested for intellectual disability and for autism. Never take it for granted that everything is fine.

Parents of late-talking children are often not only anxious but also puzzled, because pediatricians or others who examine the children may be unable to find anything abnormal that could explain why they're not talking. Even an internationally recognized authority on late-talking children, Professor Dorothy V. M. Bishop of Oxford University, says one form of late talking that professionals call "specific language impairment" is "puzzling precisely because it occurs in children who are otherwise normally developing, with no hearing problems or physical handicaps that could explain the difficulties."[12] When their IQs are measured, leaving out language aspects in which they are obviously below par, their IQs "fall within broadly normal limits." Nevertheless, with such children, their "first words may not appear until 2 years of age or later."[13]

Despite the fact that medical causes are not found to account for late talking in most children, a thorough medical examination should nonetheless always be completed by a pediatrician or family physician to ensure that no medical conditions are causing the late talking. A number of medical conditions, including hearing problems, genetic conditions such as "fragile x," and neurological conditions such as cerebral palsy or seizures, could be causing or contributing to the late talking. In most cases, no genetic or neurological conditions are found, but you can only know that after an examination, so all late-talking children should *always* be given a thorough medical examination.

One little boy named Kevin was brought to our clinic when he was three years old. He was a bright child—his IQ was 128—but his language understanding and speaking were far below age level, more like those of an 18-month-old. When I was testing him, Kevin would sometimes freeze momentarily, staring off into space. After a few seconds, his attention would return to the pictures I was showing him. Many late-talking children will look away when they do not want to answer test questions or when they are thinking, but I noticed that Kevin's eyes would not move at all when he was staring into the distance. I referred him to a neurologist, who diagnosed seizure disorder and prescribed medication that stopped the petit mal seizures he was having. In less than a year, Kevin's talking and understanding caught up completely with his peers.

It is noteworthy that another clinician before me had tested Kevin and diagnosed him as having "autism spectrum disorder"—and did not refer him to a neurologist. After the boy's seizures were treated, what had looked like symptoms of autism disappeared completely. Kevin was an example of children who at some point neither speak nor seem to understand much of what is said to them, but who nevertheless end up without any long-term problems arising from the late talking. My son is another. So, while the distinction between late-talking children who understand what is said and those who do not is important, it is not ironclad proof of anything for a particular child. While most of the former tend to turn out better than most of the latter, some who understand what is said may still have some serious problems and some who do not may turn out fine. That's why both need to be thoroughly examined by qualified professionals.

There is even a special segment of late-talking children whose intellectual development is visibly and precociously higher than that of most other children their age. They have what has been called the "Einstein syndrome," covered in chapter 5.

Many parents of late-talking children are often baffled because they have never heard of a child like their own, who is perfectly fine or even above average otherwise but does not talk when other children the same age are talking. In fact, there may be more such children than there seem to be. Many people who went through such a stage as a small child have forgotten all about it and, after they grow out of it, their parents simply heave a sigh of relief and have no reason to mention it in later years.

Because so few clinicians follow a given child over a long period, there is little or no "institutional memory" about these children's development. Clinicians may have treated such children for decades, without having treated any particular child more than a few years—and usually the same few years at the same ages for their young patients in general.

After the children have outgrown the late-talking stage, they more or less disappear from the radar screens of professionals and laypeople alike, so that many parents of today's late-talking children have no readily available information on the existence, much less the development, of people who were late talkers in the past and are now doing just fine as adults.

A mother who may be beside herself with both anxiety and puzzlement over her late-talking child, and who has never heard of such a child before, may be unaware that one of her neighbors, friends, or even close relatives went through a similar phase. Whenever I have discussed children like this in an audience of some size, someone has usually stepped forward to say they were like that or some member of their family talked late.

It may be worthwhile for the parents of a late-talking child to ask older relatives if they know of anyone in their family who was unusually late to begin talking and who was of average, or perhaps above average, intelligence. Although it is relatively rare for a late-talking child to have a sibling who also talks late—one of many signs that this condition is not due to the parent's child-rearing practices—it is more common for an uncle, an aunt, or a cousin to have passed through a similar phase.

A number of public figures are known to have been late talkers. These include Ramanujan, a mathematical prodigy from India; Nobel Prize–winning physicist Richard Feynman and Nobel Prize–winning economist Gary Becker; outstanding mathematician Julia Robinson; distinguished economist Richard Rosett; as well as famed 19th-century pianist Clara Schumann and internationally renowned 20th-century pianist Arthur Rubinstein. Novelist and diarist Virginia Woolf is also rumored to have been a late-talking child. The legendary British prime minister Winston Churchill had a lifelong speech disorder and is thought to have been a late-talking child too. We don't know for sure, but the reports that he was a rebellious and independent student when he started school would certainly fit the profile of the late-talking child being strong willed. And Dick Armey, a longtime U.S. congressman and former majority leader of the House of Representatives, was a late-talking child who went on to get a PhD in economics and teach at the university level before going into politics. Landmark figures in nuclear physics who talked late include Edward Teller and Albert Einstein as well as Dr. Feynman.

Among the population at large, an estimated 7–10 percent of all children have a type of late talking that professionals call "specific language impairment."[14] The research of others, as well as my own years of dealing with such children, has revealed some of their general patterns.

Characteristics of Late-Talking Children

One of the very basic things we know is that the great majority of late-talking children are boys. That is true not only of the patients I have seen in my clinical research program over the years; it is also true of the children in the informal organization of hundreds of families around the world mentioned in chapter 1.

Of the 608 late-talking children in these families for whom we have data, 523 are boys. Because this is a group that was self-chosen, they cannot necessarily be considered a representative sample of late-talking children in general. However, other studies of late-talking children likewise show most are boys. A large-scale study of specific language impairment by Professor Bruce Tomblin and colleagues found boys outnumbering girls by approximately two to one.[15] Studies by others show similar ratios, usually ranging from two to three boys for every girl.[16] Whatever the reason for this, the fact is undeniable.

Another of the known, but unexplained, common characteristics of late-talking children is that they also tend to be late in becoming toilet trained. While most children become toilet trained when they are two or three years old, my experience has been that this usually happens a year or so later with late-talking children. Data from another study of late-talking children found a similar pattern.[17]

Although we don't know the cause or have a cure for this yet, its practical consequence is that parents of such children need to be aware that preschools often require a child to be toilet trained before they'll admit them. However, if you are unable to get a late-talking child into a preschool, that may not be a bad thing. Although many "experts" are convinced that early socialization outside the home is essential, with this as with early intervention, everything depends on the particular child and the way the child is treated during early intervention. A child who cannot talk with either the other children or the adults in charge may not be helped, and may in fact be harmed, by being placed in circumstances with which he or she is not yet equipped to cope.

A study has found that preschool children do not select late-talking children as favorite playmates as often as they do other children.[18] It is also possible that an unusual child may be picked on by others—and be unable to tell the adults in charge about it.

For example, a late-talking boy named Adrian from Maryland was being harshly disciplined by his teacher, who was holding him against the wall while shouting at him. But Adrian did not have the ability to tell his parents or anyone else about what was happening. The situation only came to light after another parent witnessed one of the teacher's tirades and told Adrian's parents. When confronted, the teacher said that Adrian needed this kind of discipline to behave properly in class and to learn to speak. Naturally, I told the parents to take him out of that school immediately and find another that treated the students under their care humanely. Many teachers are wonderful, but some are not. And, unlike other students, late-talking children may not be able to tell their parents what is happening in school.

One characteristic of late-talking children that is not quantifiable, but that is nevertheless widely reported by parents and confirmed by my own observations, is that they tend to be "strong-willed." This too has practical implications. One is that it can be especially difficult to accurately diagnose a young late-talking child, who may simply refuse to do something asked of him or her by the person attempting to make a diagnosis, even when the child is perfectly capable of performing the task used to test him or her.[19]

Refusing to do something is interpreted by too many people who test or evaluate children as meaning the child *cannot* do it, instead of the child *will not* do it. Unanswered questions from a checklist may be counted as if they were wrongly answered, leading to a diagnosis reflecting nothing but the rigidities of the diagnosis and the unrealistic assumptions of the person conducting the evaluation. An unreliable diagnosis that results from this approach can be worse than none, when it grossly underestimates the child's intelligence and prescribes treatment based on that wrong conclusion. Moreover, that wrong diagnosis can be entered into the child's permanent records and follow him or her for years.

My own response to a child who is too uncooperative to test properly is to postpone the test, either to another day or to whatever future time will allow the child's maturity to reach the point where a meaningful diagnosis can be made. That may be weeks or months or, in some cases, even years later. Some late-talking two- and three-year-olds may not cooperate with intelligence testing until they are five or even six.

An example that comes to mind is a late-talking little boy from California who was three years old when we first saw him in our clinic. He was tall for his age and very coordinated: he could kick a soccer ball and bounce it off his head almost as soon as he could walk. A psychologist who had tested his intelligence before he came to our clinic had diagnosed him as having intellectual disabilities, because he failed to point to items on the intelligence test when asked to do so—a failure to do the assigned task being interpreted as an inability to do it, rather than an unwillingness to do it.

When I tried to test the same boy, he became agitated, pulling my necktie and biting it! I took that as a sign that he wasn't ready to be tested, so I discontinued the test. I told his father that I didn't know how smart his son was, because he wasn't mature enough to be accurately tested—and that this little fellow shouldn't be tested until he became mature enough. Better to have no intelligence test at all than to have one whose results would be completely unreliable. It was three years later, when this boy was six years old, before I was finally able to test him—and found that his IQ was actually above average.

Another trait of many late-talking children is that they tend to be more analytical than verbal.[20] Even after they begin to talk, they tend to learn better from reading than from listening—and tend to learn best of all from hands-on activity. Moreover, when most late-talking children get interested in a problem, they prefer to pursue it until they master it. For example, when some late-talking children get interested in a puzzle, they often stick with it for hours, days, or even weeks. When they are engrossed in the puzzle, they often ignore other activities and may not respond to what is said to them. Later, after the puzzle has been solved, they may quickly lose interest in it and move on to other things.

This way of learning may be fine for these youngsters but it conflicts with the way many schools are run, so it is good for parents to be alert in advance to problems that can result when their child reaches school age. A late-talking child may not want to leave an intriguing problem when the bell rings or when the teacher says it's time to put away their math book and start a new subject.

Being strong-willed, late-talking children often do not comply well with fixed periods of time dedicated to particular subjects, since they prefer sticking to a topic until they master it. The child's learning style—studying something until they've figured it out—is a mismatch with the teaching style of many preschools and elementary schools that feature learning by rote memorization and by listening. Parents need to be able to anticipate this conflict. They also need to understand the potential this creates for turning a child off from school, which can become a lifelong handicap in a world where education is increasingly important to one's prospects.

Options should be considered before such a situation arises, because there may not be a solution if the school rigidly insists on its own methods. A parent aware of this potential for conflict before it manifests itself has the option of investigating alternative public or private schools beforehand, to find one whose approach is not so rigid, or find a particular teacher who seems more flexible. In the case of preschool, there may be an option to keep the child home, rather than let the rigidities of a highly structured classroom turn the child against education early on, with lasting negative consequences.

Too often, a bored and restless child in such a setting can be labeled as having an "attention deficit hyperactivity disorder" and can have medication prescribed—drugging the child being an easier option for some schools than changing methods that are frustrating and boring for students, provoking behavioral problems. I have seen this happen many times over the years.

Causes of Late Talking

Although no one knows why some perfectly healthy children are years behind others when it comes to talking, others talk late for reasons that may be painfully obvious: severe intellectual disabilities, autism, hearing impairment, or other serious problems.

It is the late-talking children who have none of these severe handicaps—such as those late-talking children with "specific language impairment"—who are a puzzle to parents and professionals alike. Yet science has begun to get some preliminary knowledge about special patterns among such children, and these findings seem to point toward some possible causes and away from others.

The development of modern technology that enables scientists and scholars to see which parts of the brain are activated by various tasks has provided clues to which parts of the brain usually control which parts of the body and which kinds of thinking. Moreover, this brain-imaging technology also allows observers to see how these patterns of neural control and activity differ from one person to another and from one group to another. It has, for example, been known for some time that these patterns usually differ somewhat between males and females, and that the right hand is controlled from the left side of the brain and vice versa.

For most people, speech is controlled from the left side of the brain. But some studies have found that, among people with specific language impairment, a majority had speech controlled from the right half of the brain.

In the United States, a brain-imaging study of children, ranging in age from two to seven years old, concluded in 2003: "Children with speech delay have lateralization in the right hemisphere, and children with normal speech have lateralization in the left hemisphere."[21]

A 2008 study of young adults with specific language impairment in Britain found that roughly 55 percent had their speech controlled from the right side of their brains and another 27 percent had their speech controlled from both sides of their brains.[22] In other words, more than four-fifths of these young adults in Britain who had specific language impairment also had brains organized somewhat differently from the way brains are organized in most others.

These findings were not only striking in themselves, they are also consistent with other findings, using other methods. For example, an autopsy of the brain of Albert Einstein, the most famous late talker, showed his brain to be no heavier than the average brain but that one nonlinguistic part of his brain's left hemisphere was much larger than in most other people—and spread out, into the part of the left hemisphere from which speech is usually controlled.[23] We can't be sure whether this was why he was late in talking, or whether his speech was controlled from the other side of his brain, as happens with specific language impairment. But the finding is suggestive.

If the truth lies in this general direction—that a different organization of the brain is a factor in the slow development of speech among people otherwise normal—it highlights how grotesque the efforts are of some clinicians to force children into talking before their brain is ready.

Although much attention has been focused on those late-talking children with specific language impairment, others who are late in talking—or never develop the ability to speak—may have entirely different problems, such as severe intellectual disabilities, autism, or hearing impairment. The 2008 study in Britain, for example, found that most children diagnosed as being on the autism spectrum did not have their speech controlled from the right side of the brain, but from the left side, like most others.

Science is still advancing slowly and carefully toward deciphering a complicated situation. Only charlatans and zealots claim to have all the answers.

There are gender differences, not only in the way brains are organized but also in the ways different parts of the brain mature in young children.[24] There are also differences between men and women in which parts of the brain are activated by various activities. For example, in a test that asked women and men to identify words that rhymed with each other, a certain region on the left side of men's brains was activated, while regions on both sides of women's brains were activated.[25] Similarly, when males and females perform mathematical tasks or tasks involving spatial visualization, such as reading maps or doing geometry, there are different neural activation patterns in men and women.[26]

In general, control of certain activities tends to be more localized in particular parts of men's brains than in women's brains, making men more vulnerable to local damage in the brain, such as by injury, surgery, or stroke. Research has shown that women often recover the ability to speak after brain surgery or after a stroke more readily than men do.[27]

What may be particularly relevant to late-talking children is that when women and men are talking, their brains function somewhat differently.[28] Whether that's why fewer girls than boys are late talkers is a matter of speculation, but the evidence is suggestive. Not only has research found that the internal organization of brains is somewhat different between males and females, other research has shown that various mental abilities are also different, on average, between the genders, though there is much overlap. Males tend—again, on average, though not universally—to excel in mathematical reasoning and in things that require spatial visualization.[29]

Females tend, on average, to excel in reading and writing fluency and in processing speed, which is the ability to rapidly and accurately complete tasks of moderate difficulty. Boys and girls have similar overall IQs, but often have different strengths and weaknesses.[30]

Biological factors in late-talking children are also suggested by the fact that delayed speech development seems to run in families—and, more specifically, families with certain other characteristics. In my international group of families of late-talking children, of the 608 children whose parents filled out questionnaires, the fathers of more than half these children worked in analytical occupations, including engineering (134) and computer science (133). Contrast this with the percentage employed in these occupations in the overall US population. The most generous estimates from the U.S. Bureau of Labor is 19 million—out of a total labor force of approximately 150 million—or less than 13 percent.[31] Mothers were not nearly as concentrated in these kinds of jobs, although 36 mothers were engineers and 53 worked in computer science. Among the paternal grandfathers of the children in my group, 94 were engineers, and among their maternal grandfathers, 111 were engineers.

An earlier study of the families of late-talking children likewise found the families they come from tend to have an unusually high concentration of people working in such analytical occupations as engineering, mathematics, statistics, accounting, and science, including computer science and medical science.

A tabulation of the occupations of the parents, grandparents, and aunts and uncles of the children in the book *The Einstein Syndrome* showed that 35 percent of these children had at least one of these close relatives working in computer science, 20 percent had some other kinds of scientists among these relatives, along with 53 percent whose close relatives included accountants and 60 percent whose close relatives included engineers.[32] Altogether, 86 percent of the children in that study had at least one close relative in a list of analytical occupations that also included mathematicians, pilots, and physicians. Moreover, 65 percent of these children had two or more close relatives in the various analytical occupations on that list.[33]

The families of late-talking children have also had an unusually high concentration of people who play a musical instrument. Among the 608 children in my survey, 269 of the mothers played a musical instrument, while 178 of fathers did, and there were a total of 88 professional musicians among the parents. Although this means that approximately 8 percent of the parents were musicians, this is a much higher percentage than in the general population. The U.S. Bureau of Labor reported a total of 170,000 professional musicians and singers in the U.S., this is only about 0.1 percent of the overall labor force of 150 million.[34] The children themselves are rarely tested for musical ability, so we have no way of estimating the prevalence of such talents among them.

Again, similar findings were reported in an earlier study of late-talking children, where three-quarters of the children had at least one close relative who played a musical instrument. That included 57 percent who had multiple musicians among their close relatives. In just over half the families of these children, at least one parent played an instrument. Professional musicians were close relatives of 26 percent of the children surveyed in that study.[35]

In addition to evidence that late-talking children tend to come disproportionately from families with unusual concentrations of particular kinds of abilities, and that the brains of these children are often organized idiosyncratically, there is other evidence of the influence of heredity.[36]

In 2008, Dr. Karin Stromswold (MD and PhD) said in the prestigious *New England Journal of Medicine* that "children with specific language impairment are four times as likely to have a family history of the disorder as are children who do not have such an impairment."[37] Moreover, the rate at which one identical twin's late talking was also found in the other twin was almost twice as great as was the case with fraternal twins.[38] Differences between identical twins and fraternal twins is one of the indications of a trait being genetic, since identical twins have identical genes, while fraternal twins share only some genes, as with other siblings. In short, the study conducted by Dr. Stromswold and her colleagues was a smoking gun, in terms of linking language development in general, and late talking in particular, to genetics.

Despite this and other evidence that genes are factors in language development patterns, Dr. Stromswold also pointed out the difficulties in trying to isolate a particular gene or set of genes as causes. So, although it is clear that late talking is related to genetics, at this time the genes that predict whether a child will talk late are not known.

Much of what we see in our clinical research program is in keeping with the various scientific studies of delayed language development. Many late-talking children who come to our clinic have a father or mother who was also late in talking. It is also not unusual for a parent to learn from their relatives that a grandparent, uncle, aunt, or cousin was a late talker. Language development is a complex behavior, and learning to talk is the result of an interaction between learning, brain architecture, and genetics. Also, because there are probably multiple genes associated with learning to talk, it is unlikely that a single gene is responsible for late talking. There is also a link between genetics and high intelligence, so the Einstein syndrome is almost certainly related to genes, though which particular genes is as yet unknown.

Some Special Afflictions

In addition to late-talking children with specific language impairment, there are other late-talking children with afflictions that can interfere with their learning to speak at the same time as other children, or ever. Hearing problems that cannot be corrected and severe intellectual disabilities are obvious examples. Among children with severe or classic autism—as distinguished from children diagnosed as being mildly "on the autism spectrum," or "high functioning autism" which I get into in the next chapter—some will never speak. One of my painful duties is having to inform the parents of such children that the chances are only about 50–50 that their child will ever say anything. I can only imagine how much more painful it is for them to hear such news. But, fortunately, it is not something I have to say very often.

Apraxia

Among the special afflictions that may delay or prevent a child's ability to speak is a condition called *apraxia*. It is a rare condition, especially among children, but unfortunately too many late-talking children are falsely diagnosed as having apraxia. According to *Dorland's Medical Dictionary*, "Apraxia is a disorder caused by damage to specific areas of the cerebrum, characterized by loss of the ability to execute and carry out learned purposeful movements, *despite having the desire and the physical ability to perform the movements*"[39] (emphasis added). In other words, there are things some people are physically capable of doing—and in fact do automatically, as if by a reflex—but cannot do when they try to do the same thing deliberately. This condition was first discovered a hundred years ago among some adult stroke victims.

An example may make this condition clearer. One of the rare children with apraxia I have encountered was a four-year-old girl from Toronto who was brought to our clinic at Vanderbilt University. She rarely produced any intelligible words. When she tried to speak, she would grimace and could make only whining and groaning sounds. When I first walked into the room to meet her, she looked at me and said "Hi" perfectly. I then turned around and walked out of the room while waving to her and she said "Bye" perfectly.

I returned a short time later and began testing her. During the testing, I asked her to say "Hi." She looked at me and grimaced while moving her mouth. But she was unable to say "Hi" when she wanted to. I then asked her to say "Bye"—and once again she struggled to move her mouth but could only make squeaking noises.

This problem was not confined to speech. She was playing with a jack-in-the-box kind of toy, which had Mickey Mouse, Donald Duck, and other Disney characters that would pop up when she pushed the button for the particular character. While playing, she spontaneously used her right index finger to cause whatever character she wanted to pop up. But when I was testing her and asked her to "touch the Mickey button," she reached for the toy, using a closed fist, and could not make any character pop up.

Although I have seen many late-talking children who choose not to do something they are asked to do, which can lead some clinicians to the false conclusion that they are incapable of doing it, this was a very different situation. This little girl was obviously struggling to do what I had asked her to do but simply could not do it by an act of will, even though she was physically quite capable of doing it spontaneously or as a reflex reaction. True apraxia is rare among children, though some adults who have had strokes may suffer the kind of damage to their brains responsible for this condition.

Apraxia is a dire condition and the long-term prospects of someone with it are often daunting. But, as with autism spectrum disorder, many children are diagnosed as having "developmental apraxia of speech" who do not have apraxia. Despite medical definitions that have been employed for decades, some clinicians label many late-talking children as having apraxia who do not meet the medical criteria. Dr. Karen Forrest at Indiana University reviewed the criteria clinicians use to diagnose "developmental apraxia of speech" and found that these were inconsistent and sometimes contradictory and noted that "These results are consistent with the general ambiguity of the diagnostic criteria of DAS and suggest that no single deficit is used among clinicians."[40] Such inconsistent and controversial diagnoses lead to questionable treatments, including some treatments that would have little effectiveness even if the child did have apraxia.

Among these questionable treatments are oral muscle exercises, stimulating the tongue with an electric toothbrush, rubbing a child's face with ice, and other practices apparently designed to strengthen or coordinate the muscles used in speech.[41] But people with apraxia already have the muscular strength and coordination to perform various actions, including speech, as shown by their spontaneous performance of those actions, despite an inability to do so deliberately when they are asked to.

Once, while addressing an audience of pediatricians, speech pathologists, and psychologists at Johns Hopkins University, I showed them a brief video of a middle-aged man with apraxia. Then I asked the audience: "How many of you have ever seen a child like that?" Not one hand went up. "Then why are you diagnosing children as having apraxia?," I asked.

Hyperlexia

Another condition that is too often misconceived, and there-fore wrongly diagnosed, is *hyperlexia*. Here is how two leading authorities defined it: "Children whose word recognition skills are developed to a point significantly higher than expected (expectation being estimated from their general level of intellectual functioning) are called hyperlexic."[42] But word recognition skills are not the same as word *comprehension* skills. Hyperlexia is a precocious ability to recognize and read words without understanding what they mean.

Someone may recognize the phrase "magna cum laude" and be able to say it, without knowing what any of those words mean. But, because the words are in a foreign language, nobody calls that hyperlexia. However, if children are precociously good at reading words in their own language but have no idea what the words mean, that's hyperlexia. What makes hyperlexia important in the diagnosis and treatment of late-talking children is that many of these children begin to read, sometimes better than most children their age, even though their speech development lags behind that of their peers.

What's also very important is that hyperlexia is often found among children with autism, some of whom have a "compulsion to decode written material without comprehension of its meaning."[43] As a result, a false diagnosis of hyperlexia can increase the chances of a false diagnosis of autism.

In determining whether someone truly has hyperlexia, everything depends on whether they understand what they read—and that can be especially hard to find out when a child is not talking. Clinicians looking for things regarded as symptoms of autism can seize upon early reading when a child is also late in beginning to speak. The fact that such children's ability to speak has not yet developed to the point where they are able to explain what words mean—even if they know—increases the dangers of a false diagnosis.

To me, a child's early reading—with comprehension—is a very positive thing. But parents who bring their children to our clinic have told us of other evaluators who were not overly concerned *until these evaluators learned the children could read*! That can raise the specter of hyperlexia—and, implicitly, autism—if no test is performed to determine whether the child knows what the words being read mean.

In our clinic, we have developed ways of testing whether children understand what they read, even when they're not yet talking. But some clinicians who're simply going down a checklist of symptoms of autism may automatically check hyperlexia as one of those symptoms. Worse yet, some unproven "treatments" for hyperlexia have been marketed.

What You Can Do

Given the current state of knowledge, what can be done, what cannot be done, and—most important—what should not be done? These questions are addressed in detail in chapters 6, 7, and 10.

The most important thing to do when a child is late in talking is to find out whether anything is causing the delay. There are so many possible reasons, and the stakes are so high, that you cannot simply assume anything. When seeking treatment, be aware that there are many controversial, unproven, and even potentially harmful approaches. Ask questions and insist on answers supported by facts. You are entitled to specific reasons for a particular diagnosis and for a recommended treatment. Never be talked into, or worse, bullied, into a label or treatment you disagree with.

3 Late-Talking Children and Autism

When I first began seeing patients more than 30 years ago, it was rare for any late-talking child to be diagnosed as autistic, and so there would have been no need to include a chapter on autism in a book about late-talking children. But this situation has changed dramatically in recent years. In addition to being a medically defined condition, autism has now become a "social movement" wherein social, legal, and political factors are increasingly having a direct—and indirect—impact on clinical practice.[1] Now it is much more likely that a late-talking child will be diagnosed as having autism. This alarming trend is the result of a "perfect storm" combining a vastly expanded definition of autism and a national push to identify children earlier and earlier, increasing the chances that a late-talking child will be identified, or worse, misidentified, as having some form of autism.

In fact, autism is not a subtle condition. Because it is as blatant as it is debilitating, few mistakes should be made when diagnosing autism. Fortunately, the overwhelming majority of late talkers do not have autism. Indeed, *although almost all autistic children are late talkers, not all late-talking children are autistic!* But, as straightforward as this might seem, parents seeking answers about their child's late talking are increasingly hearing about autism as a possibility.

Thus, parents of late-talking children, and clinicians diagnosing and treating these children, need to know about autism and how it differs dramatically from other forms of late talking. This chapter will give you a good idea of what autism is, and more importantly, what it is not. It also surveys changing diagnostic practices from the time autism was first discovered in 1943 to the present and includes brand-new diagnostic guidelines.

What Is Autism and Where Does Late Talking Fit In?

The definitions of autism have changed over the years, making it difficult to determine whether much-publicized claims of an increasing incidence of autism reflect a real change in the number of people with this condition or are simply the result of labeling more and more people as autistic.[2] The expanding definition of autism means that today's incidence reports include many people who would not have been counted when autism was first defined and brought to public attention by Professor Leo Kanner of the Johns Hopkins University Medical School, back in 1943.[3]

Among the defining characteristics of children with autism, Professor Kanner said, are an "inability to relate themselves in the ordinary way to people," living as if "in a shell," "happiest when left alone," and having "an *anxiously obsessive desire for the maintenance of sameness.*"[4] Professor Kanner described the reactions of these children on entering his office:

The children's *relation to people is altogether indifferent.* Every one of the children, upon entering the office, immediately went after blocks, toys, or other objects without paying the least attention to the persons present. It would be wrong to say that they were unaware of the presence of persons. But the people, so long as they left the child alone, figured in about the same manner as did the desk, the bookshelf, or the filing cabinet.[5]

Autism was originally called "infantile autism," because it becomes evident in infancy, even though it lasts a lifetime. As autism became more widely recognized throughout the medical profession, by 1980 a formal description of infantile autism found its way into the third edition of the official *Diagnostic and Statistical Manual of Mental Disorders*, known as DSM-III. As some leading autism scholars described it,

IA [Infantile autism], as defined in the DSM-III, is an early onset (before the age of 30 months) disorder characterized by 1) pervasive lack of responsiveness to other people; 2) gross deficits in language development; 3) peculiar speech patterns, if speech is present at all; 4) bizarre responses to the environment; and, 5) an absence of delusions, hallucinations, loosening of associations, and incoherence as in schizophrenia.[6]

At that time, all five of these conditions had to be met for a child to be diagnosed as autistic, with the cornerstone trait being a *pervasive lack of responsiveness to other people*. In short, the diagnosis of autism always required a severely reduced or nearly complete lack of social motivation and bizarre responses to the environment. Kanner noted these bizarre responses were centered on a strong compulsion for sameness and repetitive behavior.

Because of later expansions of the definition of autism, today even children who are quite social may now be diagnosed with "autism," or "autism spectrum disorder" which wasn't the case 20 or even 10 years ago. Now, when children display *all* these traits, clinicians often describe this as "classic" autism, "Kanner's" autism, full autism, or "autistic disorder" (AD). If your child is diagnosed with autism, be sure to ask the clinician whether they think your child has classic autism, because children who exhibit some, but not all, of these autism characteristics may be described as "on the autism spectrum." Having classic autism and being on an autism spectrum are not necessarily the same thing.

Differences between Classic Autism and the New "Autism Spectrum"

A traditional diagnosis of autism required that a child simultaneously display serious deficits in behavior, *and* social skills, *and* overall development in addition to being late talking. So a child who simply started talking late, but was otherwise typically developing, would never have been diagnosed as autistic. But for an "autism spectrum" diagnosis today, the criteria are much less stringent. This is a special—and very serious—problem for late-talking children and their parents. In fact, the overwhelming majority of late-talking children do not have autism and should not be treated as if they do.

As obvious as that distinction might seem, a substantial majority of the late-talking children who arrive at our clinical research program at Vanderbilt University have already been labeled by others as being on the autistic spectrum. And it is also very common for "ASD" (the acronym for autism spectrum disorder) to have been suggested to their parents, even when there was no official diagnosis of ASD. Our own evaluations of these children conclude that many do not have classic autism, though some do, of course.

A broader concept of the "autistic spectrum" can be problematic in diagnosing and treating late-talking children. In fact, using a "spectrum" with overly broad limits has great potential for spreading confusion and needless anguish—and for providing too much latitude for clinicians whose diagnoses have been contradicted by the later development of the children they've diagnosed and labeled.

This "latitude" also makes it difficult to develop effective treatments because children with only one or two traits of autism are lumped together with children who have all the traits. Those with only a few traits are much more likely to get better than those with all the traits,[7] and they require much different treatment than those with all the autism symptoms.

This can lead to confusion and conflicting reports. Professor Cathy Lord, a leading researcher on autism at Columbia University College of Physicians and Surgeons, conducted a long-term study of children with classic autism. She and her colleagues reported that nearly all these children continued to demonstrate symptoms of autism 5 or even 7 years after having been first diagnosed and even after receiving intensive treatment. These results have led most autism experts to view autism as a lifelong disabling condition.[8]

A 13- to 22-year follow-up study of 120 people diagnosed with autism was completed in Sweden by Professor Eva Billstedt and her colleagues at the University of Göteborg. This study yielded similar findings: the overall outcome was "poor" in 78 percent of the cases. Only four of the participants lived independently (3.3 percent), and even these "good"-outcome patients reportedly lived "isolated lives."[9]

Contrast this with reports on children on the "autism spectrum." An article titled "Aging Out of Autism" appeared in the February 4, 2013, issue of *Time* in the Health and Science section. The authors reported that "some children who receive behavioral intervention to treat autism might be able to age out of their symptoms, outgrowing them like last year's shoes."[10] The scientific paper this news story was based on appeared in the *Journal of Child Psychology and Psychiatry* in February 2013.[11]

The "optimal-outcome" children in this paper did not have classic autism and in fact had normal or above-normal IQs. The diagnostic criteria used in their case included the following:

"early language delay (no words by 18 months or no phrases by 24 months documented in the report was required) along with an ASD diagnosis by a psychologist or physician specializing in autism." In short, they had a normal IQ, talked late, and had been identified as having ASD. I have no way of knowing how many symptoms of autism the children actually displayed when first diagnosed. The authors of the scientific paper are skilled clinicians as well as credible scientists and there were no attempts at deception in the paper: they reported that the children in the study were "high functioning" and "ASD" rather than saying the children had classic autism. Despite this, the *Time* article was titled "Aging Out of Autism" and the crucial distinction between traditional autism and ASD is blurred in the news story.

It's clear that the children in this report have fewer and less severe symptoms than those in the articles on classic autism by Professor Lord and by Professor Billstedt. Is it any wonder that they also have much better, "optimal" outcomes? Yet, readers may mistakenly confuse the children in these studies when both are simply identified as having "autism." Worse, a parent whose child has all the symptoms of classic autism may mistakenly believe that their child is like those who had an optimal outcome and "aged out" of the autism symptoms, when in fact their child is much more likely to grow up with severe disabilities like the children in the studies by Dr. Lord and Dr. Billstedt.

There is additional recent research that demonstrates the important difference between diagnosing classic autism and a much broader "autism spectrum disorder." When a child is diagnosed with classic autism, the long-term stability of the diagnosis is very high. That is, if a two- or three-year-old is identified as having all the symptoms of autism, follow-up studies conducted years later show that more than 90 percent of these children still have classic autism.[12]

In stark contrast, only about one-third of the children initially diagnosed as having "autism spectrum disorder" maintain that label in follow-up testing in later years.[13] The odds of correctly diagnosing classic autism in a two- or three-year-old are very high, but on a broader, less stable "autism spectrum," these odds are much less than 50–50. Yet, despite this huge difference, it is not unusual for clinicians to lump all children into "ASD" and use the label "autism" and "ASD" interchangeably, as happened in the *Time* article on optimal outcomes. That's why it's very important to ask whether a late talker being diagnosed as "autistic" is viewed as having classic, full-blown autism or as simply having one or two symptoms of an "autism spectrum disorder."

Imagine the problems that would be created if a child could be diagnosed as being "on the blindness spectrum." This "spectrum" could cover everything from not being able to see at all to simply needing glasses or even slight myopia. Imagine the needless alarm that could be spread among parents when they heard such a dire diagnosis. Imagine the vast sums of money that could be drained away from helping genuinely blind people to be spent on a vastly larger number of other people, whose only problem is that they need glasses. Also imagine the latitude that a concept like "on the blindness spectrum" would provide for a clinician who made that diagnosis for a child who later turned out to have 20/20 vision with glasses.

No human, even the most skilled clinician, is infallible. A broad "autism spectrum" should never be used to as insurance against a more dire initial diagnosis of autism that later proved untrue, any more than telling a parent that their child would never be able to see would justify using a more nebulous "blindness spectrum" if that child turns out fine later on. If a clinician is diagnosing autism spectrum disorder, parents have every right to know why this diagnosis was made and whether their child has only one or two, or all, of the symptoms of autism. And no parent should ever be accused of being "in denial" when these questions are asked. Skilled clinicians welcome questions from parents and take the time to explain their findings as well as the reasons for their diagnosis.

During his lifetime, Professor Leo Kanner's prestige as the discoverer of autism enabled him to throw his weight against the broadening of the definition of that term. He opposed what he called the "habit to dilute the original concept of infantile autism by diagnosing it in many disparate conditions which show one or another isolated symptom" of autism.[14] "Almost overnight, the country seemed to be populated by a multitude of autistic children," he said. "Mentally defective children who displayed bizarre behavior were promptly labeled autistic."[15] After Professor Kanner's death in 1981, one of the defenses against ever-widening definitions of autism was gone.

Children who are genuinely autistic have many needs, and the direct and indirect costs of trying to meet those needs can put a severe financial burden on their parents. Just the fact that one parent may have to quit working to take care of an autistic child is a major indirect cost. The funds available from government programs or from private philanthropic organizations to provide some much-needed help to these children and their families should not be dissipated on the vastly larger number of children who are not classically autistic, but who can be labeled as being on a loosely defined "autistic spectrum" and will likely "age out" of the symptoms anyway.

There's another danger in the misapplication of the concept of an "autistic spectrum." That's the illusion that we've reached the point where some people can cure autism. We can all fervently hope that that time will come soon, but it's not on the horizon today. However, there's nothing easier than to "cure" children who were never fully autistic in the first place, and whose natural development took them to the point where they simply outgrew the behaviors that met the broad definition of being "on the autistic spectrum."

Another unfortunate side effect of the ever-widening "autism spectrum" is that the herculean determination needed to teach a child with classic autism is sometimes grossly underestimated by those dealing with children on the more nebulous "autism spectrum." I have seen families with bright and shy children who are otherwise functioning very well (and who have been placed "on the spectrum") giving advice to parents of classically autistic children that trivializes the magnitude of what the family of a child with severe autism is trying to cope with. Telling the family of a child with classic autism "when she gets upset, just reason with her" reflects a very naive view of what classic autism actually entails. I have also seen clinicians with experience treating "high functioning" patients who are at a complete loss as to how to treat children with classic autism.

New Guidelines for Diagnosing Autism Spectrum Disorder

In the spring of 2013, the American Psychiatric Association published new guidelines on the diagnosis of autism spectrum disorder. These guidelines are published in the fifth edition of the APA's *Diagnostic and Statistical Manual* (DSM-V). The categories "Pervasive Developmental Disorder–Not Otherwise Specified (PDD-NOS)" and "Asperger Syndrome" have both been dropped as diagnostic categories. This is very good news because many late-talking children have been mistakenly diagnosed with these conditions.

Another piece of good news is that simply being socially immature or awkward is not supposed to put a child in the autism category any more. But, the unfortunate news is that the overall autism category is now called "Autism Spectrum Disorder," which codifies the broader autism spectrum. The stable, accurate label "Autistic Disorder" is now gone as well, having been rolled into the Autism Spectrum Disorder diagnosis. Now, when an autism spectrum diagnosis is made, the clinician must decide if the child meets the specific traits listed in the manual and must then rate the severity. So, children with classic autism will be rated as "severe," while those with fewer traits who are "high functioning" will be rated as mild. Parents now need to specifically ask the clinician diagnosing their child how severe they think the autism spectrum disorder is. I also advise parents to ask which traits are being used to make the diagnosis. Late talking alone, and any symptoms that can be accounted for simply because the child is not talking, are not sufficient to warrant an autism spectrum diagnosis.

In addition, a new category titled "Social Communication Disorder" has been added in the DSM-V manual under the rubric of communication disorder diagnoses. The APA defines this social communication disorder as characterized by a persistent difficulty with verbal and nonverbal communication that cannot be explained by low cognitive ability. Symptoms include difficulty in the acquisition and use of spoken and written language as well as problems with inappropriate responses in conversation. The disorder limits effective communication, social relationships, academic achievement, or occupational performance. Symptoms must be present in early childhood even if they are not recognized until later when speech, language, or communication demands exceed abilities.[16]

If a late-talking child is diagnosed with autism spectrum disorder, be sure to ask the clinician whether a differential diagnosis for social communication disorder has been completed and why an autism spectrum diagnosis is being made rather than a social communication disorder diagnosis. Because this is a new category, some clinicians may not be familiar with the traits and may mistakenly put these children into the autism spectrum category. It is not at all unusual for late-talking children who are not otherwise autistic to have "problems with inappropriate responses in conversation." But when there are any problems in conversation, some clinicians may automatically default to an autism spectrum diagnosis even when the correct diagnosis should be social communication disorder instead.

Finally, no late-talking child should now be diagnosed with Asperger syndrome or with PDD-NOS. These labels are not part of the DSM-V because a number of studies showed that they were unreliable and unstable diagnoses. In a paper published in the *Journal of the American Medical Association–Psychiatry* in 2011, the authors reported: "Several conclusions are inescapable. In these 12 university based sites, with research clinicians selected for their expertise in ASD and trained in using standardized diagnostic instruments, there was great variation in how BEC [Best Estimate Clinical] diagnoses within the autism spectrum (i.e., autistic disorder, PDD-NOS, and Asperger syndrome) were assigned to individual children."[17]

In short, the authors concluded that there was insufficient stability in Asperger and PDD-NOS diagnoses to warrant including these categories in the new DSM-V. Because the clinicians in this study were highly trained and worked within strictly controlled research environments, it is likely that these autism spectrum diagnoses have been even less reliable in the field. The removal of these ASD categories may bring small consolation to families of late-talking children who were previously misdiagnosed. But at least their needless anguish should not be repeated in the future. If parents receive either a PDD-NOS diagnosis or an Asperger syndrome diagnosis; this indicates that the clinician is not using current diagnostic guidelines. Parents are advised to seek an evaluation from a clinician who uses the current guidelines.

Early Diagnosis: Benefits and Pitfalls

The difficulty of diagnosing autism can vary greatly, depending on the age at which the diagnosis is made. When a child is four or five years old, making the diagnosis is relatively easy. At this age, autism is unmistakable and readily identifiable. Empirical studies confirm this. The long-term accuracy of an autism diagnosis in five-year-olds is very high. And this is one reason that autism diagnoses were so rare in late-talking children when I first started practicing more than 30 years ago: autism was diagnosed after age four, five, or even older so that late-talking children who were going to catch up anyway had already done so and were not mistakenly diagnosed with autism.

Of course, both parents and clinicians would rather have autism discovered much earlier, so treatment can be started when it might be more effective. The problem is that the earlier the diagnosis is made the less reliable it may be. Many young toddlers go through phases when they do some of the same things children with autism do—of which not talking is just one.

Although severe cases of classic autism—as originally defined by Kanner—can indeed be recognized in the first year of life by skilled clinicians, it is not unusual for all two-year-olds to do things such as throwing tantrums, which children with autism are also notorious for doing. That's why people speak of the "terrible twos" in all children, whether late talking or not. Toddlers often repeat the same routines, as children with autism are inclined to, and some toddlers are also notorious for ignoring peers and parents when pursuing their own interests. But many odd things toddlers do at this stage are simply regarded as cute—except when these toddlers are also late in talking, when the very same oddities are then viewed as "symptoms" or "red flags" to justify an autism spectrum diagnosis.

When a toddler talks late, he or she can easily be mistakenly identified as being on the autism spectrum, if the clinician doing the diagnosis is not sufficiently skilled, experienced, and open-minded to realize that a behavior that would be a red flag with an older child, is in fact just one of the phases many toddlers go through. The persistence of a transient behavior in an older child is often a diagnostic marker for autism, but not necessarily an autism marker for a younger child.

Despite the adoption of universal screening of children for autism at a very early age in the United States as part of a plan to initiate "early intervention," in Britain the British Health Service has recommended *against* the screening of two-year-olds for autism. Everyone—whether parents or professionals—wants children screened for autism as soon as a reliable diagnosis is possible. The disagreement is about how early accurate screening can be done. A 2011 report appearing in *Pediatrics* entitled "Early Autism Detection: Are We Ready for Routine Screening?" concluded "On the basis of the available research, we believe that we do not have enough sound evidence to support the implementation of a routine population-based screening program for autism."[18] Having seen repeatedly how much damage can be done to children and parents alike by unreliable diagnoses, I share the British Health Service's misgivings about screening all two-year-olds for autism, even though the American Academy of Pediatrics recommends autism screening at 18 months and 24 months in their guidelines for preventative pediatric health care.[19]

This is not to say that I am in any way opposed to testing—and diagnosing—toddlers, or even younger children who display core autism symptoms or are otherwise at risk. As noted in chapter 2, all late-talking children should receive a medical examination and be evaluated for autism and intellectual disabilities. Skilled clinicians *can* accurately diagnose autism in toddlers.[20] But, unlike a simple hearing or vision screening, this takes careful observation and interacting with a child in a variety of activities, which is simply not possible in a quick screening process.

The simple truth is that nearly all late-talking two-year-olds will likely fail an autism screening because being unable to speak is by far the most obvious marker for autism. But because most late-talking children do not have autism, *accurate* universal screening is problematic. Any child who fails an autism screening test should not be labeled until *after* a thorough diagnostic assessment has been completed that *conclusively* establishes that the child does indeed have autism. And the evaluation should be completed by an experienced clinician who is not simply seeking to confirm the results of the autism screening.

Another problem for universal screening is that late-talking toddlers are not the only children who exhibit behavior common among autistic children. Children with unusually high IQs—"gifted children"—often have behavior patterns similar to those found among children with autism. Research published by Professor Ellen Winner of Boston College, in her book *Gifted Children*, detailed some of these patterns. According to Professor Winner, it is not unusual for gifted children to "show high persistence and concentration when they are interested in something" and have "almost obsessive interests in specific areas, such as computers." They also "show unusually intense reactions to noise, pain, and frustration."[21]

Gifted children "refuse to submit to any task that does not engage them and, as a result, often end up labeled as hyperactive or with an attention deficit disorder." In addition, they "often play alone and enjoy solitude" and "seem to march to their own drummer."[22] Like the autistic man in the movie *Rain Man*, many gifted children "are fascinated with number and number relations" and have "prodigious memories."[23] Anyone eagerly looking for things that could be considered symptoms of autism can certainly find them in gifted children. Indeed, there is a special class of late-talking children who also show signs of unusually high intelligence, even while they are not yet speaking. These children are described in Professor Thomas Sowell's book on the Einstein syndrome[24] (I discuss this syndrome in chapter 5). If they are like other gifted children, in addition to not talking, they are doubly in danger of being falsely diagnosed as being autistic or on the autistic spectrum.

The Autism "Epidemic"

Many parents come to our research clinic at Vanderbilt University out of fear that their late-talking child is part of the autism epidemic often reported in the U.S. media. It's certainly true that the number of people diagnosed as autistic has increased dramatically over the years, both absolutely and as a percentage of the total population. In 1976, the rate of autism was reported as between four and five cases per 10,000 people, which means about one per 2,000 to 2,500 people.[25] The rate of autism was reported as one in 400 in 1995, one in 150 in 2001, one in 90 in 2007, and one in 88 in 2012.[26] The most recent estimate in 2014 was 1 in 68 overall and 1 in 42 boys! Worse, these figures do not include the recent implementation of Universal Screening for Autism. so it is likely that the "incidence" will double or even triple in the next few years as more and more late-talking children are mistakenly identified with Autism Spectrum Disorder. The media and some professionals have called this an autism epidemic. Those crusading for early diagnosis and intervention have used such numbers to buttress their arguments. So have those crusading against various chemicals in the environment as a supposed cause of autism.

Some people have argued that there has been a real increase in autism. Others have argued that autism has simply been detected more often, as a result of greater awareness or earlier diagnoses— in other words, that there was always more autism than people realized, and now more of it is being detected. Still others have argued that the increase is more apparent than real and attribute it to changes in diagnostic approaches. They suggest that the trend toward broader definitions,[27] as well as the increasing willingness of clinicians to diagnose children as autistic or on the autism spectrum, have resulted in more diagnoses than before.

One study concluded, "The proportion of children with an autism code increased from 12.3/10,000 in 1996 to 43.1/10,000 in 2004; 51.9% of this increase was attributable to children switching from another special education classification to autism (16.0/10,000) ... diagnostic substitution accounted for at least one-third of the increase in autism prevalence over the study period."[28] Another study argued, "In general, there has been a broadening of the criteria and a recognition that there is a spectrum of autistic conditions. This encompasses a range from 'classical' (Kanner) autism, through to Asperger syndrome or 'high-functioning' autism (current evidence suggests that the latter two are the same condition), and can include more anomalous conditions called 'pervasive developmental disorder—not otherwise specified' (i.e., the presence of similar behaviours, but at a level below the threshold for diagnosis). This leaves plenty of latitude for researchers and clinicians to make varying interpretations from their diagnostic assessments, and it greatly widens the capacity to accept children with social, cognitive and behavioural problems and what might have been called 'eccentricity' in former times, as being 'on the spectrum." Thus, diagnostic practices will be a contributor to the increasing identification of cases."[29]

Empirical evidence strongly suggests that there has been a limited, but real increase in what Leo Kanner originally defined as autism, and what is today called classic autism. Its incidence has remained remarkably stable at about one in 400 children over the past decade.[30] Another striking fact is that, as the number of children diagnosed with autism has risen, the number diagnosed as intellectually disabled (what used to be called mentally retarded) has declined—and by very similar numbers.[31] This too suggests that changes in definitions and in diagnostic practices are contributing to the perceived "epidemic" of autism.

Why is this important for late-talking children and their parents? If a late-talking toddler is identified as being on the autism spectrum, early intervention services are offered by school systems and others. After the age of three, a child is eligible to be placed in special education classes in preschool in their local school district. In some states, insurance will cover part or all of the costs of treatment, and there are also government-funded programs that treat children who have been diagnosed as autistic. The existence of these programs creates incentives for many professionals to label late-talking children as autistic or on the autism spectrum, which can lead to financial support for treatments. But many of these treatments can create serious problems for late-talking children who do not have autism, instead of being beneficial.

When the parents of a late-talking child take their three-year-old to their local school district to be evaluated for enrollment in preschool, *what the parents are seeking and what the school officials are seeking have quite different purposes*. The parents want a diagnosis for their child that will explain why he or she is not yet talking. But the school officials evaluating the three-year-old want to know what kind of program the child may be *eligible* to enroll in. The parents' problem is compounded if they accept what the school officials offer for their child when that program does not address the actual diagnosis.

The child may not be autistic by a *medical* definition of autism or even the broader autism spectrum disorder category. But, under the law, state school districts can establish their own criteria for placing a child in a program for children with autism. In fact, I was once involved in a case where I demonstrated that the child did not meet a medical definition of being autistic, but the school district's psychologist showed that the child met the district's definition, which was all that was needed to place the child in that school's autism classroom. Fortunately, I was able to get that particular child taken out of the program for children with autism. But I was not able to get the school district's policy changed, so other children could still be put in an autism program that did not fit their real condition. Schools evaluate whether a child is *eligible* for special education, *not* whether a particular diagnosis is correct. Many parents I have seen over the years have been dismayed and confused when autism is ruled out by a physician or psychologist, but their late-talking child is subsequently found to be eligible under an autism label by the school and then assigned an autism classroom.

School programs often use techniques that may be appropriate for children with autism that can disrupt the normal development of children without this condition. Moreover, a diagnosis of autism can have a dramatic—and negative—impact on the way teachers view and treat a child. A false diagnosis of autism can even affect the natural interaction between parent and child, on which so much else depends.

If a late-talking child does in fact have autism, it is vitally important that the condition be accurately diagnosed and that effective treatment be delivered as early as possible. Because autism is a dire lifelong condition that requires great amounts of efforts by parents and a huge investment of money for professional treatment, whatever money is available for children with autism should go to children who are genuinely autistic—and not be dissipated on large numbers of other children who have simply been given an autistic spectrum label because of overly broad criteria. I admire the herculean efforts I have witnessed in families providing for their children with autism. They need all the help they can get.

What You Can Do

Always rule out autism in a late-talking child by having a qualified clinician do an assessment. If a late-talking child is identified as having "autism spectrum disorder," parents should ask the following questions:

1. Have other conditions, such as social communication disorder, language disorder, or speech disorder been ruled out?

2. How severe is the autism? Does my child have classic autism?

3. Is the purpose of the assessment to diagnose autism or simply determine whether my child is eligible for early intervention or preschool services?

4. Do you think my child will grow out of the autism? Do you think my child will ever go to regular school? If so, when?

5. What percentage of the late-talking children you see end up with an ASD diagnosis? Do you believe that some late-talking children catch up on their own? What are the odds that my child will catch up?

6. If my child was talking, would you still diagnose him with autism? What symptoms other than late talking led to an autism diagnosis?

Clinicians should be happy to answer these questions and to explain the reasons for the diagnosis provided. If your child does have autism, contact Autism Speaks, autismspeaks.org. This is an outstanding advocacy group, which will likely have a local chapter that includes other families whose late-talking child has autism. You'll also find helpful information on the group's website.

4 Lessons from Autism: Charlatans, False Causes, and Questionable Cures

Parents of late-talking children—and the clinicians treating these children—can learn from the horrible experiences encountered in autism. There have been, and continue to be, false causes and cures for autism that are pushed on families and clinicians.[1] As more and more late-talking children are mistakenly put on the autism spectrum, it is increasingly likely that false causes and worse, questionable cures will be imposed on them as well. As described in chapter 2, many late-talking children eventually catch up without treatment. Because of this, there are many opportunities for superstitious causes and cures to arise. A clinician misidentifying a late-talking child as having autism or some other dire condition will have a very high "success" rate—so long as the "cure" does nothing to retard a child's natural development.

Although the overwhelming majority of clinicians working with autism spectrum disorders and with other forms of late talking such as speech disorder and specific language impairment are outstanding, parents need to know how to detect those offering false causes and questionable cures.

So, in addition to the distress parents struggle with and the difficulties health professionals encounter in treating this condition, there have been further complications and heartbreak from a whole series of supposed "cures" for autism offered to desperate parents. There is no known cure. However, that has not stopped a variety of false "cures" from being promoted, not only by charlatans, but even by some earnest healthcare professionals eager to find something to offer children with autism and their desperate parents. Some of these professionals have let their hopes outrun the hard evidence. A few have even defied hard evidence that shows some "cures" to be not only futile, but counterproductive or even dangerous.

Parents who come to our clinical research program at Vanderbilt have described some of the quack treatments they have been urged to try or have actually resorted to. My research on autism, and my work on a National Institutes of Health committee that reviews other people's research, have made me painfully familiar with many of the "cures" that come and go over the years. It would take too much space to try to cover all of these bogus treatments and "cures" here, so I'll mention just a few. Parents who are urged to subject their child to procedures their common sense warns them against may find those questionable treatments covered in a book titled *Autism's False Prophets* by Dr. Paul A. Offit, who holds an endowed chair as a professor of pediatrics at the University of Pennsylvania Medical School. Another excellent book that unmasks quack treatments for autism is *Defeating Autism: A Damaging Delusion* by Michael Fitzpatrick, a physician from the United Kingdom. His experiences as a parent seeking treatment for his own son with autism provides firsthand experience with the false claims all too often pushed on parents.

Among the bogus treatments for autism that I have learned about from patients at my clinical research program is a process called *chelation*, used to remove mercury and other metals from a child's body on the theory that mercury or other toxins cause autism. There is no evidence that autism or any form of late talking is caused by mercury either in vaccines or from other environmental exposure. But this doesn't stop some clinicians and even some physicians from recommending chelation as a treatment for autism. A scientific panel working with the US National Institutes of Health reviewed autism treatments and stated unequivocally: "There is currently no medical or biological treatment of the core features of ASD."[2] In plain English, there is no drug, vitamin, special diet, or brain training computer game available currently that can cure autism.

Quack Cures

But be forewarned, successful charlatans can readily provide a convincing rationale to support their "cures" for autism even in the face of a complete lack of credible scientific evidence. A physician in Oregon writes: "Chelation works like the body's natural sulfur defense system, wherein sticky molecules bind toxic metals to sequester and eliminate them."[3] He then states: "Chelation helps break many of the self-perpetuating cycles contributing to the tissue damage and symptom complex of autism and opens the way for apparent recovery to take place." And he also writes: "If your child has been diagnosed with autism, and particularly if he/she has regressed or lost skills from an earlier stage in life, it is extremely likely that environmental factors have caused the injury. In the DAN [Defeat Autism Now] group, we believe that genetic and probably epigenetic (gene switching due to environmental influences) predispositions interacting with toxic exposures cause the syndrome of autism." This physician concludes with: "May the day come when your child thanks you for all your efforts in bringing the best of biomedical treatments to facilitate his or her recovery!"[4] This statement certainly sounds convincing and firmly rooted in medical science even though it is sheer nonsense: Just a few years after this was written, the US Food and Drug Administration issued a recommendation against using chelation as a treatment for autism.[5]

But, I have seen firsthand how powerful and persuasive spurious causes and cures, such as the chelation "treatment" for autism, can be—especially when parents are desperate for answers. A little boy from a southeastern state came to our clinical research program at Vanderbilt University. His mother, a nurse, was very concerned about what his late talking could mean. Prior to visiting us, she had also received an independent opinion from a physician. After completing the evaluation, I told her that her son would probably catch up within a few years or even faster. I later learned that the physician had said the same thing: both the physician and I believed that he would catch up before too much longer.

About a year later, this mother contacted me and was very upset. She told me that another physician had diagnosed her son with poisoning from "toxins," including lead and mercury and that her son required chelation as a treatment for his late talking. This mother then reported that she watched the metals pour out of her son and that, thankfully, they caught the toxic exposure in time to prevent serious damage. Finally, she told me that her son had now begun talking much more than when I had seen him and generally was doing well *because* of the chelation treatment. It turned out that she was quite angry that I did not "do something" to help her son and that I should have referred her to the charlatan!

Understandably, she was very anxious about whether the positive predictions the first physician and I had made would come true. She was naturally concerned there was something seriously wrong with her son. Because it is clear from scientific evidence that chelation is not a proper treatment for autism or any other form of late talking, it is highly unlikely that either the charlatan or the "cure" had, in reality, helped her son. But even a mother with professional medical training fell victim to worry and the need to "do something," which overwhelmed her common sense. After she finished berating me, I told her that I was very happy that her son was doing well regardless of how it happened and that I was very pleased that the chelation did not appear to have harmed him, which sometimes can happen. The FDA report on chelation in autism included this sobering warning: "FDA is also concerned that chelation can result in serious side effects such as dehydration, kidney failure and death."[6]

But there was simply no convincing her that anything other than chelation therapy had "fixed" her son's "problems." Even when I pointed out her son had gotten better exactly as her physician and I had both independently predicted, she remained adamant that only the heroic actions of the chelation doctor had saved her son.

Unfortunately, the coincidence that her son caught up after the "treatment" bolstered her staunch belief in the quack "cure." I wonder if she ended up telling other parents about her son or referred other families to the charlatan. As a nurse whose late-talking son was now much better, she could well be a very credible witness in persuading other parents of the virtues of chelation therapy as a cure for late-talking children. Despite her sharp criticism of my advice, I am sympathetic to her plight: I could not supply the certainty the charlatan did. And, after all, from her point of view "seeing is believing," and her son did talk much more after the "cure." She has a great personal and financial stake in validating her son's treatment. However, I am much less sympathetic to the charlatan's point of view. In light of his medical training, he should know better than to prey on a patient's fears in this manner.

This child had a happy ending because he caught up and, as far as I know, had no long-term consequences from the late talking—or negative effects from the chelation therapy. Although I detest the needless fear—and needless expense—this family and other families like them go through, it is far worse when a late-talking child really does have autism because the promises of a "cure" never materialize. The parent's very real fears are preyed upon and scarce financial resources needed to help the child are squandered.

Chelation treatment had been used on a boy in Minnesota before he was brought to our clinical research program at Vanderbilt University. He has severe autism spectrum disorder in the full and classic sense—as distinguished from being "mildly on the autism spectrum." At the age of seven, this boy still does not say any words at all, and instead uses a picture book to communicate. For example, when he wants milk, he'll point to a picture of a glass of milk in the book, and he'll point to a picture of a DVD player when he wants to watch a movie, and so on. It is understandable that his father, desperate to help his little boy, has tried all kinds of "cures," including chelation, that did not work. The sad fact is that doing so lost valuable time in his son's early childhood, when we (or others) could have been teaching him some of the things that can be taught to children with autism to ease their problems and their families' problems.

Embracing fake modes of treatment for autism is not a new problem. In 1997, Dr. Patricia Howlin from St. George's Hospital Medical School in London lamented the lack of evidence for questionable treatments in autism. The list included special diets, vitamins (including B12 shots), listening programs such as "auditory integration therapy," riding horses, specialized motor exercises and massage, and even one approach that recommended holding the child tightly until they became agitated.[7]

Facilitated communication (FC) is another discredited treatmentwherein the clinician "facilitator" helps a child type messages on a keyboard when the child cannot speak for themselves. Unfortunately, the "messages" actually originate from the facilitator rather than the child. Worse, there have been a number of terrible cases wherein children were taken away from parents based on false accusations of abuse. The charges were always proved untrue when examined scientifically. A pediatrician wrote: "The optimistic side of FC, that nonspeaking children could miraculously become competent communicators, is unfortunately a myth. The dark side of the phenomenon of FC includes false hope, false communication, family disruption, losses of job and reputation, and inappropriate use of scarce resources."[8]

Sadly, these discredited approaches seem to get get recycled under new names with slight alterations and pushed onto a new generation of families seeking answers. For example, Facilitated communication is now being repackaged as "supported typing," but remains a controversial, discredited treatment. There are no shortages of quack treatments which have plagued families over the years. Unfortunately, these approaches are still thriving today.[9]

False Causes

There are false "causes" of autism, as well as false cures. One of the most infamous falsehoods grew out of a 1998 article in the distinguished British medical publication *The Lancet*, where it was claimed that certain vaccines cause autism—a claim that *The*

Lancet itself later repudiated.[10] The sample on which that claim was based was 12 children.[11] As someone who teaches statistical analysis, I know that a sample of 12 can seldom prove anything. This particular sample was also completely biased, because several of the children were selected and provided by a lawyer suing vaccine manufacturers.

Later studies by scientists in medical institutions in several countries, including scientists at the Centers for Disease Control in the United States—and using samples ranging as high as more than half a million children in Denmark and two million children in Sweden—found *no* evidence that vaccinations caused autism.[12] There was no higher incidence of autism among children who had been vaccinated than among children who had not been vaccinated. That should have been the end of that theory. But it was not. Too many people had too much invested—emotionally, financially, or otherwise—to abandon the antivaccine movement.

That movement has remained committed to its crusade and denounces people like Dr. Offit, who has long urged vaccination and has publicly refuted claims that vaccinations caused autism. Here, as in other cases, a wrong conclusion is more than simply an intellectual error. There are serious, real-life consequences. As the *Washington Post* reported in 2010,

The Lancet medical journal formally retracted a paper Tuesday that caused a 12-year international battle over links between autism and the childhood vaccine for measles, mumps and rubella.

The paper, written by British doctor Andrew Wakefield, [suggested] that the combined shot might be linked to autism and bowel disease.

His assertion, now widely discredited, caused one of the biggest medical rows in a generation and led to a steep drop in vaccinations in the United States, Britain and other parts of Europe, prompting a rise in measles cases.

Data released last February for England and Wales showed a 70 percent surge of measles cases from 2007 to 2008, most because of unvaccinated children.[13]

In 1998—the year in which Wakefield's paper appeared in *The Lancet*—there were 56 cases of measles in England and Wales. By 2008, there were 1,370 cases.[14] Some children have died.[15]

Like many false claims, the claim that certain vaccines cause autism is based on a half-truth—and half-truths can be more dangerous than lies, precisely because of a factual component that makes the whole theory look plausible. In addition to vaccines themselves, thimerosal, the mercury compound used to preserve them, was also blamed for causing autism. The truthful half of the half-truth is that there is no question that an excessive amount of mercury in our bodies can have devastating effects on the brain and causes neurological symptoms. Indeed, the phrase "mad as a hatter" is based on the muscle tremors, slurred speech, and hallucinations 19th-century hatmakers displayed after prolonged exposure to mercury compounds used to produce hats.[16] But another old saying—"It is the dose that makes the poison"— applies here.[17] In other words, *how much* mercury matters.

The amount of mercury used in modern vaccines is a fraction of what it used to be, and it has been removed completely from most vaccines since 2000. But even the older vaccines did not create the dire consequences now being warned against. Moreover, which mercury compound is used also matters, since the body rids itself of some mercury compounds and accumulates others. But all such scientific considerations are ignored by those who simply take the idea that mercury is dangerous and run with it. Some do so out of ignorance. Others do so because they have a vested interest in a particular treatment or approach, or are lawyers who sue pharmaceutical companies that make vaccines.

What should be the final chapter in this painful vaccines-cause-autism episode came in May 2010, when the *New York Times* reported: "A doctor whose research and public statements caused widespread alarm that a common childhood vaccine could cause autism was banned on Monday from practicing medicine in his native Britain for ethical lapses, including conducting invasive medical procedures on children that they did not need."[18] The General Medical Council applied its most severe sanction against the doctor, Andrew Wakefield, 53. Dr. Wakefield had abandoned medical practice in Britain in 2004 as questions intensified about his research and set up a center to study childhood developmental disorders in Texas, despite not being licensed as a physician in the United States.[19]

Although it would seem that this should end the vaccines-cause-autism theory and the unproven treatments based on that theory, it is not at all certain that it will, because Dr. Wakefield is by no means alone in promoting that thesis. Zealots who have appeared on popular TV programs to publicize their message seem unlikely to abandon their beliefs, and those profiting by charging parents high prices for treatments based on those beliefs may be equally unlikely to give up this theory.

Several celebrities have also been promoting the vaccine-autism hoax. Model, author, and TV host Jenny McCarthy has widely claimed that vaccines caused autism in her son and that she cured him by following a strict diet, providing vitamin supplements, and detoxing his body of metals. Even though it is now well known that Dr. Wakefield's theory was a scientific hoax and all these "treatments" do not cure autism, Ms. McCarthy was quoted in a July 2013 article on the Business Insider website as continuing to argue that vaccines cause autism: "Without a doubt in my mind, I believe that vaccinations triggered Evan's [her son's] autism." She added: "Following bio-medical treatment—which is basically changing the diet, giving vitamins and supplements and detoxing the body from metals or candida [yeast/fungus infection]— and he recovered. And the reason the medical community has such a hard time with this is because we are treating and healing a vaccine injury ... this is truly a revolution."[20] Sadly, there will still be parents willing to try almost anything that promises to help their autistic child, and they are the most vulnerable to false causes and quack cures.

At this point, medical science cannot supply what parents of children with autism most desperately want: An explanation and a cure. Charlatans can readily supply both. Moreover, whatever science can say about particular issues, such as whether vaccination has any effect on the autism rate, it can say only with varying degrees of confidence, based on the particular statistics analyzed. Even if science can say that its conclusions have a probability of 99.9 percent, that's still not absolute certainty. But charlatans can offer certainty—and zealots can offer certainty combined with a venting of pent-up emotions against presumed villains, accused of putting vaccine makers' profits above the well-being of children.

Again, consider what Ms. McCarthy had to say about pharmaceutical companies making vaccines in the July 2013 Business Insider article: "The reason why [the medical community] is reluctant to talk about it is because there's such a huge business in pharmaceuticals." This follows an even stronger statement appearing in a 2009 interview in *Time*: "I do believe sadly it's going to take some diseases coming back to realize that we need to change and develop vaccines that are safe. If the vaccine companies are not listening to us, it's their f___ing fault that the diseases are coming back. They're making a product that's s___. If you give us a safe vaccine, we'll use it. It shouldn't be polio versus autism."[21]

Moreover, charlatans and zealots can provide the kinds of flesh-and-blood examples that can be paraded on television. This is something that statistical probabilities cannot compete with emotionally, even if those probabilities are based on studies of millions of children and the examples shown on TV may be only a handful, arbitrarily selected to try to prove some point, and presented with rhetoric more concerned with its emotional impact than with its factual accuracy.

Parents are understandably outraged after they have been led to believe that their child's dire condition is due to someone's vaccine; and led to believe that people who deny the vaccines are the cause are just sacrificing their child to vaccine makers' profits. This can happen no matter how unsubstantiated or unscientific the charge is. Sometimes the net results of all this are not only bad consequences for the children and increased stress for the parents, but also death threats made to scholars or reporters who publicize facts that many do not want to hear or to let others hear.[22]

To understand why some parents are willing to try unproven, or even disproven, treatments for their autistic child, we would have to understand their desperation. After all, they live every day with a child whose growth and development are quite different from other children and with whom they can't readily establish the usual human relationships other parents have with their children. I understand the desperate plight of parents who try these things in the hope of finding a cure. One mother of a child with classic autism told me she was going ahead with chelation treatment, even after I'd explained the treatment was questionable and had risky side effects, because, in her words, "I don't want to look back and say I left any stone unturned in trying to help my son." She added: "I believe what you're telling me about chelation, but if there's any hope at all, I want to go ahead." Of course the chelation accomplished nothing. But luckily in this case, it doesn't appear to have harmed him.

But precisely because the parents are so desperate, health professionals should never add the cruelty of false hopes to these parents' other burdens, or subject helpless children to stressful treatments that may even set back whatever progress they are capable of.

Even false treatments that may be harmless in themselves can do serious damage by absorbing time and money better spent improving the lives of children with autism and helping their families. And, of course, measures like preventing children from being vaccinated risk diseases that can be devastating or even fatal. It is understandable that parents may want to leave no stone unturned in helping children with autism or preventing others from becoming autistic. But turning over some stones can let loose dangers lurking underneath.

One sign of both the desperation and dedication of many parents of children with autism came to me after CNN broadcast a feature about our clinical research at Vanderbilt University. Some parents who watched that program got the impression that I can cure autism and deluged our clinic with phone calls. Some of these parents offered to move to Nashville, to make it easier for me to treat their child. Imagine what a sacrifice that would mean: giving up jobs and breaking local ties with friends and family, just to help their child have a chance at a better life! It pained me to have to tell these dedicated parents that neither I, nor anyone else I know of, can cure autism.

What does cause autism? The plain fact is that scientists don't know yet. But quite a bit is known, and new discoveries are made every year. For example, scientific research has suggested that genetics plays an important role.[23] Studies of identical twins show that when one twin has autism, the other also has autism in about 60 percent of the cases. But, with fraternal twins, when one twin has autism, the other is autistic only 10 to 25 percent of the time. Comparing identical twins with fraternal twins is a common test for the effect of genes on any number of characteristics, such as blood type or hair color, since identical twins have the same genes, while fraternal twins have only some genes in common, as with siblings in general.

Although it is clear that autism does run in families, the specific gene or genes, and the specific process by which they lead to autism, remain among the mysteries that science is working on but has not yet solved.[24] Moreover, genes are not the whole story, or else the identical twin of someone with autism would always have autism too.

It is also clear that brain development is unusual among people with autism, so that individuals with autism have trouble processing what they see and hear,[25] including language, and trouble understanding the many social cues normal people receive and respond to automatically and almost unconsciously. As a result of brain-imaging technology, some children with autism have been found to have abnormalities in some parts of the brain. But this is not true of all children with autism. Similarly, some autistic children have relatively large heads but many do not, and it is clear that *not every child with a large head has autism!* Indeed, a review of the data on head size in autism conducted in 2013 showed that large head size is *not* a reliable marker for autism.[26]

One of the practical problems in trying to study the brains in autism is that many of these children are difficult to test. They are often unwilling to lie down in brain-scanning machinery and will often refuse to cooperate with other procedures. There-fore we cannot be sure that the children whose brains scientists have been able to scan are typical of autistim in general, rather than including mostly—or exclusively—high-functioning chil-dren "on the autistic spectrum," for example.

A study published in 2010 sought to get around the problem of noncooperation by using brain scanners in the wee hours of the morning, when children would be sound asleep. Like earlier studies, this one found atypical brain development. However, this study included children "with autism spectrum disorders,"[27] so it is still not clear how many of these children had classic autism.

In short, science has discovered certain anomalies com-mon—but not universal—among children with autism. No one can look at a brain scan or a genetic analysis and tell whether a particular child has autism. But we do know a number of fac-tors that *do not* cause autism. First and foremost, there is no evi-dence that autism is caused by poor parenting—for example, by so-called refrigerator mothers, mothers who fail to provide the emotional warmth a child needs, as some have claimed.[28] If poor parenting is the reason for autism, why would autism afflict one fraternal twin but not the other in over 75 percent of the cases?[29] Can anyone seriously believe that a mother is cold to one twin and warm to the other?

That particular theory of the cause of autism is no longer widely accepted by people familiar with the research on chil-dren with autism, but it has by no means completely died out. While I was writing this book, the mother of a child with autism came to me in great distress because she had been told her lack of emotional warmth had led to her child's autism. This particular mother happened to be a physician but, despite her medical train-ing, the charge was enough to keep her awake at night, blaming herself for the child's disability. She was greatly relieved when I explained why that theory had been completely discredited.

Another theory that is completely discredited by people familiar with the scientific evidence—but that is still going strong anyway—is the theory already mentioned that autism is caused by vaccines or by the mercury in vaccine preservatives. Such discredited theories continue to have consequences for parents and children alike. If anyone prescribes a treatment based on the assumption that autism is caused by a child having an emotionally cold mother, or because of vaccines, or because of mercury poisoning, or because of unspecified "toxins" in the environment, the validity of the treatment prescribed is questionable at best.

None of these things would account for one fraternal twin being autistic while the other is not, as is the situation in over 75 percent of the cases,[30] even though one twin is almost certainly living in the same physical and emotional environment as the other and received the same vaccination at the same time.

Because the causes of autism remain unknown, a wide variety of treatments flourish, based on a wide variety of assumptions about the causes. Some of these beliefs are based on what experience or science has revealed. Other beliefs—and the treatments based on them—continue on in defiance of both experience and science.

Dangerous Charlatans

Sadly, Andrew Wakefield is not alone in promoting quack theories about causes and cures; there has been a long history of autism crusaders who popularized a particular cause or cure that subsequently was debunked, but only after much harm had been done. Internationally known psychiatrist Bruno Bettelheim, for example, blamed autism on "refrigerator mothers" for failing to provide enough emotional warmth. The fact that an influential professional would make such a reckless and devastating claim, without any real evidence, is one sign of the many minefields parents of late-talking children have to cross.

Bruno Bettelheim's career also highlights another great danger when desperate and trusting parents turn their children over to a charlatan. Dr. Bettelheim was internationally renowned, and after his death in 1990, obituaries praised not only his clinical work but also his reputation as a humane and almost saintly person who ran residential institutions for children diagnosed with severe problems, of which autism was just one.[31] But that reputation became a bitter mockery when former patients and even former colleagues and disciples came forward after his death to paint a radically different picture of him as someone who conducted a reign of terror among the children entrusted to his care, arbitrarily inflicting both physical and verbal abuse.

One of the earliest exposés appeared in the *Washington Post*, written by a freelance writer named Charles Pekow. Pekow had spent a decade as a residential patient under Dr. Bettelheim and cited his own and others' experiences. Others came forward to describe abuses in the same institution:

"Those who were going through normal adolescent growing pains were labeled as psychotic," said Alida Jatich, a Chicago computer programmer and former inmate. ... I often saw Bettelheim drag children across the floor by their hair and kick them. He even hit autistic children who couldn't speak clearly. ... Roberta Redford, who spent her late adolescence at the school and is now an Ohio office manager, said he called her a "slut" for putting pictures of the Beatles on the wall. Often Bettelheim used all-school assemblies to tear people down; once he used the forum to tell a boy that his father had asked to have him committed for life. ... Bettelheim himself often walked into bathrooms where teenaged girls were undressed, Redford said. Jatich said that Bettelheim once pulled her out of a shower and beat her, wet and naked, in front of a room full of people.[32]

Newsweek magazine reported that not only former patients but even former colleagues and followers now came forward to describe what Bettelheim was really like:

Patients were not the only ones who knew of Bettelheim's explosive temper. There are indications that at least the local psychiatric community knew exactly what was going on, and did nothing. Chicago analysts scathingly referred to the doctor as "Beno Brutalheim." William Blau, a counselor at the school in 1949, explains the silence from school staff members by claiming Bettelheim was a cult figure for them. Another former teacher agreed. "He created a disturbed culture there," she says. "If he said the sky was green, he expected you to see it that way, and many of us did." As for the patients' silence, "Who would believe us?" asked Pekow.[33]

A long article in *Commentary* magazine by Ronald Angres, another former patient, detailed other examples of Bettelheim's unpredictable and sadistic cruelties. Angres said: "I learned as the years passed, he insulted people just in order to break any self-confidence they might have. In time, he broke mine very thoroughly."[34] A psychologist named Bertram Cohler, who had been both a patient at the school and later Bettelheim's hand-picked successor, said that he remembers the fear the patients felt at the sound of Bettelheim's leather shoes squeaking in the hallway as he made his nightly rounds.[35]

The old saying, "Power corrupts and absolute power corrupts absolutely," applies far beyond the realm of political power. Dealing with parents who are stressed out, vulnerable, and trusting gives too many charlatans in too many places too much arbitrary power, even if few abuse that power as badly as Bettelheim did. It should be noted that some of the people he abused at least had the ability to speak. Late-talking children are even more vulnerable when their parents are not there to protect them.

What Can Be Done

Although there have been many abuses and all too many false causes and cures, there has also been much important progress in treating autism. Indeed, the past 40 years have witnessed a complete shift in how autism is viewed. The condition was once thought of as being pretty much untreatable, and the children were all too often warehoused in institutions. Even today, in some cases—thankfully, very few—the symptoms are so severe that the family decides to place the child in an institution. No one should be critical of this decision, because some children with autism hit, bite, or otherwise injure themselves or throw such massive tantrums that families are unable to provide the care they need at home. But enough new knowledge and experience have accumulated over the years that such desperate measures are no longer required for most children with autism.

While there are limits, even today, to what can be done for children with autism, those limits vary with the child, and "high-functioning" autistic children have been able to live independently and, in some cases, have a career. One of these favorable outcomes includes Temple Grandin, a highly intelligent woman with autism who has a PhD in Animal Science from the University of Illinois. She has made a career of studying animals in her work as a professor at Colorado State University and as an agricultural consultant who, among other things, develops humane techniques for slaughtering animals. Unlike late-talking children who prefer to interact with others who share their interests, Dr. Grandin has indicated that she doesn't enjoy talking to people. She has never married or had children. Dr. Grandin has written a book about her life, *Thinking in Pictures*, and Oliver Sacks has written about her in his book *An Anthropologist on Mars*.

Another person with autism who has gone on to have remarkable achievements as an adult is Trevor Tao, who lives in Australia. Today he is a research scientist at the Defense Science and Technology Organization in Adelaide. As a child, Tao won awards for both chess and music. At age 11, he played Dvorak's "New World Symphony" on the piano without a note of music in front of him, and he went on to participate in international chess tournaments. However, all this happened only after years of dedicated work and emotionally draining efforts by a therapist named Jane Bryant, who later wrote a privately printed book titled *The Opening Door* about her experiences.

It must be kept in mind that Dr. Grandin and Trevor Tao are what are called "high-functioning" people with autism: those with extraordinary intelligence who also have autism. The movie *Rain Man* presents a very realistic depiction of such a high-functioning person.

Although most people with autism cannot currently be brought up to these levels, some things can be done to give many children with autism a much better life. There are literally hundreds of studies showing that children with autism can be taught using focused teaching methods.[36] But even achieving what is possible with our current state of knowledge requires great effort and patience on the part of both parents and clinicians. It also requires steering clear of charlatans, zealots, and bogus treatments that can waste the precious time needed for the kinds of treatment that have a track record of benefiting children with autism.

When a child has autism, parents should seek behavioral treatment to directly teach the skills and abilities their child needs to talk, to learn, and to take care of themselves. Parents should always be viewed and treated as partners in the teaching process and not as some obstacle to be overcome. Parents should also be included in selecting the skills being taught. But, even when everyone works together using state of the art treatment, some people with autism will never learn to talk and thus need to be taught to communicate using pictures, sign language or a computerized communication system like the boy from Minnesota described earlier in this chapter. Most will learn to talk, but, like Temple Grandin, may still not enjoy conversation or other forms of social interaction.

My advice to parents is to be skeptical about miracle cures. If you decide to try one of these questionable treatments, *please* check with your pediatrician or family physician to make sure the proposed treatment won't harm your child. The truth of the matter is that there are no shortcuts to a cure for autism. However, there is reason to be hopeful. All children, even those with classic autism, can learn and make progress. But the process is not quick or easy. If a charlatan offers a "quick fix" for autism using vitamins, special diets, "detox" treatments such as chelation, or special "computer training," please seek another clinician who can help you work with your child.

Fortunately, the overwhelming majority of cases of autism aren't severe enough to warrant institutionalization. Most children with autism can be taught at home and school, if everyone is willing to roll up their sleeves and work together to teach them how to talk and how to learn, using the techniques of behavioral intervention. Every child with autism must be taught step by small step, patiently and persistently.

What makes autistic children so much harder to teach than most other children is that most other children *want to have social interactions* with the people around them, but children with autism do not. Aversion to social interaction is at the heart of autism. Most children want to communicate with others, so they're motivated to begin to talk, after their development reaches the point where this is possible. But, for a child with autism who has little or no *intrinsic* desire to communicate, even when they can talk, some other, *external* motivation must be sought.

Because so much of what most other children learn comes from parents, brothers and sisters, peers, and teachers, enhancements to these spontaneous social interactions must be provided. In other words, some other motivation must be found in order to get children with autism to pay attention to what people are trying to teach. What would motivate them depends on their interests, and detective work is needed to determine which interests will induce them to cooperate.[37]

In some cases, using food as a reward is necessary, because some children won't talk or learn unless they're given candy, a cracker, or some other preferred food.[38] In other cases, a motivating activity, such as access to a computer, may produce the desired result. For example, the computer can be placed out of reach, inducing the child to communicate with a parent in order to gain access to it. Most children with autism would rather do things on their own than communicate with others, so this technique will only work if the reward—whether favorite foods or access to a computer—is highly desired by the child. The desire for the food or object must be stronger than their motivation to shy away from other people.

One mother of a five-year-old boy in North Carolina told me her son could say the word *computer* but never asked for it. He was quite resourceful and would just get on the computer by himself. When they put it out of his reach and had his father demonstrate the phrase "computer please," the little boy walked away without saying anything. The next day, however, he came to his mother in tears, and said "computer please." Now he readily asks for the computer, DVDs, and preferred food items because he can only get access to these things by talking. If left on his own, he wouldn't talk. In this case, the parents knew their son had the ability to speak, because he would sometimes say words when playing with the computer, although these words were not directed at anyone.

Caution must be used, though, to refrain from taking an object away from the child or withholding an object while prompting the child with autism to speak. It is better to arrange the environment so that the child needs the parents' help rather than snatching things away from them. This is because if things are snatched away, we are essentially teaching the child to avoid us because we'll take away their toys. The key here is to ensure the child with autism is coming to parents for help as a positive way of initiating social interaction. Another key is showing them that talking improves their lives by more efficiently gaining access to preferred objects and activities.

Note that this approach, which is reasonable when used with a child with autism,[39] can be counterproductive in other contexts or in late-talking children who do not have autism. When Professor Sowell used this approach to try to get his son to say "water," it ended with both father and son in tears. In cases where a child with autism can't speak, pictures or sign language can be used as a means of communication. As noted earlier in this chapter, a little boy with classic autism who still couldn't speak at the age of seven could nevertheless communicate by pointing to a picture of a glass of milk in a book, or to a picture of a videocassette recorder when he wanted to watch a movie. So speech, as such, although helpful, is not essential to this process. *Motivation* is.

In our clinical research program, we use words that match the pictures or sign we demonstrate to children with autism. What we are trying to do, in a more general sense, is *show the children the power of communication.* That is, we try to show them that it is to their advantage to communicate. They get what they want if they give us a picture, use a sign, or say a word. Without using force, or withholding toys or food, we make sure that nonspecific requests such as grunting, whining, or throwing tantrums are not successful.

We also try to get parents to arrange the home environment so that the child can't go through the whole day without having to communicate. We advise parents to make sure that the child can't open the refrigerator (by putting a lock on it), get into pantries (again, using a lock), turn on video or computer equipment, or go outdoors without parental assistance. In all these things, the goal is to motivate the child—in a natural and positive way—to communicate.

We don't recommend withholding things and prompting the child to ask for them, but rather making sure that to get what they want, they have to somehow make their wishes known. When a parent tries to deliberately force communication by direct prompting, often the response is a huge tantrum because the child doesn't want to communicate. One or two of these thermonuclear meltdowns are often enough for the parents to let the child get their way. We recommend that the behavioral intervention program be started with only one or two items, such as a favorite food or activity. Be patient and encouraging and add new items only after requesting the highly desired items is firmly established. After a few have been learned, most children learn new requests much more quickly. *Only* use prompts such as "say ___" if a late-talking child has autism and can readily imitate on demand. Common sense tells us that it is cruel to withhold objects or food when a child is unable to speak or imitate on demand. We conducted a study showing that children who could not imitate on demand responded poorly during treatment that relied on prompting a child to imitate. The overwhelming majority of late-talking children, including many with autism, do not respond or learn using force such as direct prompting (such as "say ___"). Unfortunately, many clinicians use prompting as a primary approach—or even the sole one—for teaching late-talking children.[40]

Many parents naturally do not want to frustrate their child at all and so let them have unrestricted access to food, toys, and computers. And, having low motivation for social interaction that is the essence of autism, the child is content to do everything alone and without communicating. But communication must be promoted as the child's magic key to getting whatever is desired, whether that communication is by words, pictures, or signs. Initially, a child with autism may resort to words solely as a means to an end, of getting what is wanted, such as a favorite food or activity. Moreover, this very restricted role of words may continue for a long time, even if the child with autism understands other uses of words.

Heartbreaking as it may be, many people with autism prefer not to converse. Even a very high functioning adult with autism, such as Temple Grandin, rarely initiates conversations. Dr. Grandin is a very effective speaker at her public lectures and will answer questions. But she usually only initiates conversations with others when she wants information. It is also noteworthy that she chose a career working with animals. I suspect she may have chosen this line of work because it does not require extensive communication with other people.

The larger point here is that growing knowledge and experience have made autism more treatable than in the past,[41] and provide reason to hope that more progress will lead to still more effective treatments and—we can only hope—a cure.

It is important to note that the approach to teaching children with autism that we recommend to parents in our clinical research program is just one of a number of approaches that can improve the lives of these children and their families. Other approaches I would recommend highly include those developed by Professors Robert and Lynn Koegel at the Koegel Autism Center at the University of California at Santa Barbara, the details of which are described in the book *Overcoming Autism* by Lynn Koegel as well as in the book *Positive Behavioral Support* by Robert Koegel. Another recommended approach is the Early Start Denver Model by Professors Sally Rogers and Geraldine Dawson.[42] Still another has been developed and tested by Professor Connie Kasari at UCLA.[43] Of course, there are many additional approaches that are well known and widely used by clinicians, some of which are effective for certain children with autism but not others. For example, Applied Behavior Analysis therapy, commonly known as ABA or "Lovaas," (named after O. Ivar Lovaas, who developed the approach), can be effective in children with autism who readily imitate when prompted to speak.[44] The common theme in all these is to *motivate* communication while also teaching the child with autism a *means* of communicating such as speaking, pictures, sign language gestures or computers. There are plenty of validated programs to teach children with autism, so parents need not resort to false causes and questionable cures offered by charlatans.

5 The Einstein Syndrome

Just as late-talking children in general tend to have some personal characteristics in common, there is a special category of late-talking children with their own special characteristics—and whose families also have special characteristics. These children are not only exceptionally bright from an early age—often noticeably brighter than average, even before they are able to talk—but their special intellectual abilities tend to be concentrated in analytical areas, in extraordinary memory, and in music. However, especially in their early years, they usually lag behind in social areas, and as with other late-talking children, their parents often report that they are "strong-willed" and also tend to be late in toilet training. But, these late-talking children do not have autism and should not be labeled or treated as if they do.

Even when they are toddlers who say nothing, such children may be able to put together jigsaw puzzles designed for older children or adults, or they may be able to figure out how to open child locks intended to keep them out of kitchens or other dangerous places. Some have been able to use computers by themselves as early as two or three years of age. Parents also report prodigious memories—sometimes described as "photographic"—among these children. When we give nonverbal IQ tests to such children, they often score substantially above average. Children like this have sometimes been described as having "the three M's—math, memory, and music."[1]

Such evidence as we have about the children's musical abilities is anecdotal. The child described in Dr. Thelma E. Weeks's book, *The Slow Speech Development of a Bright Child*, asked to learn to play the piano at age four and was given lessons when she requested them, rather than on a schedule.[2] In his book *Late-Talking Children*, Thomas Sowell mentioned his son's precocious playing of a xylophone, without lessons, even earlier—and his ability to transfer that musical talent to a piano he saw in a home they visited when he was four, also without any lessons and on his own initiative.[3]

Einstein played the violin from an early age[4] and Edward Teller played the piano as a child, sometimes for hours when he felt like it,[5] and both continued to play these instruments as adults. Professional musicians who talked late include famed 19th-century pianist Clara Schumann, who was a sensation in Europe, and internationally renowned 20th-century pianist Arthur Rubinstein. Both began playing the piano in early childhood. By age eight, Schumann could turn her back to a piano and name which of the 88 keys someone struck.[6] Rubinstein began playing the piano when he was three years old and, at age seven, gave his first public performance.[7] Both had prodigious memories.

The most famous person with extraordinary mental abilities who was nevertheless unable to speak at an age when other children could speak was of course Albert Einstein, leading to the use of the term *Einstein syndrome* to describe this unusual combination of characteristics. This is not a medical condition requiring any special "intervention." Rather, it is a form of normal development in exceptionally bright people. Until now, very little has been written about people who exhibit these traits. Weeks's book, *The Slow Speech Development of a Bright Child*, described in detail a set of special characteristics in one child that were later found in a group of dozens of children described in two books by Sowell, *Late-Talking Children* (1997) and *The Einstein Syndrome* (2001). My own clinical research has turned up examples of the same phenomenon among some of the children I have diagnosed or treated. But, as a percentage of all the late-talking children I see, those with the Einstein syndrome are a small fraction. Most late-talking children do not fit this pattern.

As with other late-talking children, once children with the Einstein syndrome finally begin talking—as Einstein did at age three and Edward Teller at age four—they usually catch up, sometimes very quickly, and the parents' anxieties subside quickly. As with other late-talking children, the net result is often that the parents' memory of this early period fades into the background with the passing years, and this phase of their child's early development is seldom mentioned. Moreover, as with other late-talking children, there is seldom any institutional knowledge of their later development by the speech pathologists, kindergarten teachers, or others who may have encountered them when their ability to speak was limited or even nonexistent.

While many people with the Einstein syndrome may show extraordinary abilities in particular areas—usually analytical and/or musical areas—they are seldom above average across the board.

There are no studies exclusively of children with the Einstein syndrome, nor are there definitive criteria. But, out of the larger group of late-talking children, there are some with such extraordinary mental skills of a particular kind that they need to be examined separately. Just as there is considerable evidence that genetics is involved in the delayed development of speech, there is considerable evidence that genetics is involved in high levels of intelligence. A study of individuals with IQs higher than 160 by Dr. Robert Plomin of King's College in London and his colleagues Professors David Lubinski and Camilla Benbow at Vanderbilt University have found a gene associated with high IQs. Using the same techniques, they say that it should become possible to identify more of the many genes thought to affect both intelligence and personality.[8]

How does all this fit together? What causes this phenomenon of children who are visibly more advanced than other children their age in some areas and yet lag behind other children in beginning to speak? No one knows at this point. What we do know is that more than 90 percent of the late-talking children in both Professor Sowell's group of dozens of families, and in my group of hundreds of families, have a close relative who is in either analytical or musical occupations—and more than four-fifths have multiple close relatives in these occupations. And, this proportion is much higher than one would expect in the general population.[9] One may speculate as to why this is so, but the fact itself is not a speculation. We have barely scratched the surface and there is much research waiting for scientists to undertake.

What could be very revealing, and very valuable, would be a long-range study along the lines of Professor Lewis Terman's famous study of children with IQs of 140 and above (titled "Genetic Studies of Genius), which followed these children for decades into their adult lives. One of the great missing pieces of information about late-talking children in general, and of Einstein-syndrome children in particular, is knowledge of how they develop in later years. Few professionals or scientists follow them for more than a small slice of their lives, so knowledge of how their later development unfolds would not only be a great addition to our knowledge, but could also serve as a check on the validity or lack of validity of the labels put on them as toddlers. I worry that the development of highly intelligent children is being derailed by mistaking their high intelligence for autism, ADHD, or some other clinical problem when, in fact, they are simply developing differently.

Many, including Einstein and Teller, were thought to have intellectual disabilities when they were young children.[10] In later times, a common misdiagnosis of children with the Einstein syndrome has been that they have autism. Anything that might restrain the unwarranted and sweeping labels too often put on children—and the needless anguish these labels cause parents, as well as the stressful and counterproductive treatments they lead to with the children—would be of great value.

As noted in chapter 2, studies of the brains of late-talking children with specific language impairment have shown their brains to be somewhat differently organized than the brains of people with typical speech development. There is also indirect evidence of various abnormalities associated with the brain among people of unusually high intellectual ability, which may be relevant to children with the Einstein syndrome.

Johns Hopkins University, for example, has long had a program studying children with extraordinary mathematical ability—12-year-olds who score 700 or higher on the mathematics portion of the Scholastic Aptitude Test, which is designed for people old enough to be entering college. More than four-fifths of these highly gifted children are left-handed and/or myopic and/or allergic[11]—some of these variations from the norm being things associated with the functioning of the brain.

Nor are these particular children unique in such patterns. Others with extraordinary mental abilities have been found to have similar differences in other functions of the brain. These include mathematicians and top-rated chess players, both of whom have a higher-than-average incidence of left-handedness and/or ambiguous handedness.[12] Among very bright children in general, a study found the rate of childhood myopia to be roughly four times the normal rate.[13] There is also a much higher incidence of allergies than normal among members of the high-IQ Mensa Society.[14] An extreme example of allergies among people with extraordinary mental ability was the British mathematical genius Alan Turing, a key figure in breaking the supposedly unbreakable Enigma code used by the German military during the Second World War. Turing's allergies were so severe that he sometimes wore a gas mask to filter out irritants in the air.[15]

Uneven learning patterns are not a trait restricted to late-talking children: There can be striking learning disabilities in some people who are unusually good at learning particular things but below average in learning other things. Unlike late-talking children, who may excel at math and music simultaneously (like Teller and Einstein), a study found that musically gifted individuals had trouble learning mathematics. They also had dyslexia and other learning disabilities, twice as often as other people in the same study.[16]

What does all this mean? The short answer is that we don't know. But what we do know is that it is not uncommon for unusually high mental abilities to be accompanied by differences in other things affected by the way the brain develops and functions. Against that background, the Einstein syndrome is not as strange as it might seem. Some neuroscientists have speculated that there is a competition for resources within the brain, especially as it is developing in early childhood.[17] They hypothesize this competition can lead to some brain functions gaining more than the normal share of available resources, at the expense of other functions.[18] But, if the brain is developing analytical ability while talking comes along slowly, this is very noticeable because it is not the usual pattern. On the other hand, most children learning to talk on time may be slower to develop mathematical abilities. But this doesn't cause alarm because the pattern of later developing math skills occurs much more frequently. If so, these different patterns of *normal* development while the immature brain differentially allocates neural assets to speaking *or* to analytical abilities could help explain some of these anomalies. But only future scientific research can provide a definitive answer.

The Einstein Syndrome in Childhood

Among my purely personal observations of children with the Einstein syndrome is that most are without guile or malice. They tend to be sweet kids—and sometimes they are targets of other kids who are not sweet, and who may resent their superior intellectual ability in school.

Teachers and school administrators are often not welcoming to Einstein-syndrome children, who create problems in a system with one-size-fits-all education. Parents tend to heave a great sigh of relief when their late-talking children finally begin to speak, but new problems often lie ahead in school. Parents need to be on guard so that these problems don't turn their child against school, thereby wasting their great potential and jeopardizing their future in a world where education is increasingly important.

The case of a three-year-old boy from Nashville who came to our clinical research program speaking only a few isolated words was all too typical of what can happen. This little boy, who I'll call "Jimmy," was recruited for a research project I ran at Vanderbilt University. We gave Jimmy a nonverbal IQ test, on which he did well, and his understanding of words was excellent, even though he spoke very few words himself. When he was three, he talked like a one-and-a-half-year-old but understood like a four-year-old. He could also add and subtract numbers. His parents described his outstanding ability to do jigsaw puzzles. Jimmy was also good with computers, which he could operate without adult help, to play educational games.

When Jimmy was taken to school to be enrolled in kindergarten, the school officials didn't want to put him in a regular class but in an autism class. He was legally eligible for the latter segregated autism classroom, due to his delayed language development and the fact that schools are allowed great latitude in determining who is eligible for placement in these classes, whether or not the children meet a medical definition of autism. I went to the school and managed to get Jimmy put into a regular class instead. But the story did not end there.

As often happens with late-talking children, Jimmy wouldn't perform on cue in class. Like many late-talking children, he was strong-willed. However, he was not defiant and was in fact emotionally vulnerable. When given an assignment he didn't feel like doing, Jimmy would just do nothing. When the teacher insisted, he would start to cry. Now he was considered to have emotional problems too, when in fact the problem was that the work the school was giving him was uninteresting to him because it was too easy. Like many children with the Einstein syndrome, Jimmy matured socially more slowly than other children. He continued to take a favorite toy with him to school, which made him a target for teasing.

In the fourth grade, the school tried to label Jimmy "behavior disordered." The reason, I discovered, was that he tore up math problems, wadded up the paper, and threw it away. Then he would stand on his desk and tell jokes. All this struck me as especially odd, since he did nothing like this in his other classes. But the math they were teaching Jimmy in the fourth grade involved fractions and decimals—which he had mastered two years earlier.

I suggested giving him geometry, since he could sit in class and quietly read a geometry book rather than acting up out of sheer boredom. But this was rejected as contrary to the one-size-fits-all philosophy prevailing in many schools. I then asked the teacher: "What would you do if I made you do dozens of elementary addition and subtraction problems?" But nothing would make the school budge. I then told them they had two choices: either give the child something to do that fit his own intellectual level or have a continuing behavior problem on their hands.

Fortunately, the family moved to another state, where the father informed me later that little Jimmy was no longer a behavior problem in his new school. Jimmy's father, incidentally, was in an accounting firm, accounting being one of the analytical occupations common among families of children with the Einstein syndrome.

When Jimmy turned 13, his IQ was 134, putting him in the top 2 percent. His numerical reasoning quotient, which measures mathematical ability and abstract numerical problem solving, was 154 by then. In contrast, his verbal ability remained below average for years, but he did eventually catch up in this area, so that his verbal ability quotient is now 105—compared to

64 when he was four years old. While a verbal ability quotient of 105 is in the normal range, it is nowhere near the level that Jimmy has reached in analytical ability. This kind of pattern is not unusual among children with the Einstein syndrome. When Jimmy was four and his verbal ability quotient was 64—far below normal—this led some teachers to underestimate his potential. But, even then, his IQ score was 126, so clearly he was much more intelligent than his verbal skills would have indicated.

After moving, Jimmy's father reported that his son attended a small Christian school, matured at a rapid rate, and made a small circle of friends he greatly enjoyed. Academically, Jimmy became an A student and his standardized test scores were consistently in the 99th percentile, with the highest scores being in math. He then attended the Duke University summer program for gifted children. More recently, Jimmy's father reported that as a high school senior, Jimmy is still socially awkward, but had a great year. He was accepted into the Georgia Governors Honors Program in Mathematics, selected for the National Honor Society and was chosen as the Star Student at his high school for receiving the highest SAT score in his class. Jimmy is now going on to Georgia Tech as a mathematics major. The dire predictions and reports of "behavior" problems in elementary and middle school are now simply a bad memory, and his father couldn't be prouder of Jimmy's accomplishments—rightfully so. But I can't help wondering if all these wonderful outcomes would have happened if the parents didn't take Jimmy out of the school that didn't believe in his abilities and wanted to incorrectly label him, or if they simply accepted the placement in an autism classroom.

Another late-talking child who came to our clinical research program was a two-year-old girl we can call "Carol." We were shown videos of her before she was brought in person—and those videos aroused our concern, because in them she was aloof and would just ignore her parents when being called. Carol spoke no words at all when she was two and a half years old. However, she scored high on our nonverbal IQ test and had a very good vocabulary of words that she understood, even though she spoke none herself. She was also exceptionally good with numbers. She began to talk when she was 29 months old, but we continued to see her every year or two, to monitor her development.

Among her idiosyncrasies was that she would sometimes rehearse words before saying them, something Einstein also did as a child,[19] as did a late-talking girl named Leslie described in Dr. Thelma Weeks's book, *The Slow Speech Development of a Bright Child*.[20] Late-talking children are often perfectionists and may not do or say something they are capable of doing or saying, if they have any doubt about doing it perfectly.[21]

Carol's father was a scientist at the Oakridge Laboratories in Tennessee, and she went into kindergarten in Oakridge at age four. There was no serious problem at the Oakridge school, perhaps because they encountered other children like Carol, given the concentration of scientists and engineers in that community. However, when her family moved to Texas, she entered a school more like many other public schools, and there the officials wanted to put her in a class for children with autism. Her advanced reading ability was wrongly labeled "hyperlexia" (unlike hyperlexics, she understood what she read), and her refusal to do some assignments reinforced the school's determination to put her in a special class. Less demonstrative than Jimmy, Carol would simply put her name on her exam paper and turn it in blank when she was not interested.

I phoned the school authorities in Texas repeatedly on behalf of this little girl. But, while the school officials in Oakridge had welcomed my input, the officials in Texas were not only resistant but tried to discredit me. They demanded to know if I had ever taught in a school, which of course I had never done, except at Vanderbilt and other universities. They questioned my professional qualifications, asking if I had read a certain study. I offered to send them my published critique of that study. They demanded to know what I knew about autism. I offered to give them my credentials and articles I had published on the subject in scholarly journals.

The special education team was quite upset when Carol's parents refused to allow her to be put in a separate school for children with autism. The officials pressured the parents, saying that it would be better for Carol to be in a school where the teachers could "meet her special needs." Fortunately, the law requires school systems to place a child in the "least restrictive environment" meeting that child's needs. So, despite pressure from the school officials, Carol's parents refused to give their consent, on my advice. The school team then worked together to educate Carol in a regular classroom—where she learned quite well.

Today, several years later, no one suggests that she be put in a separate classroom or that she would have been better off in a class for children with autism. Recently, Carol's family moved to Spain, where she qualified for admission to a selective British school in Barcelona.

A little boy from California who I'll call "Wally" was first brought to us in January 2006, at age two. He didn't speak a word. But he understood everything said to him and liked playing with other children. Speech therapists and others in California had told his parents that Wally would never be able to talk—and you can imagine what a devastating impact that had.

Our examination of the boy led to no such dire conclusion. On a nonverbal IQ test we gave him, he scored over 130, far above the norm. He could put together 12-piece jigsaw puzzles at age two. He liked LEGOs and could build houses with them. He would put little toy people and animals in the house and pretend they lived there—something children with autism don't do. Wally was also good at imitating animal noises or other sounds, so I knew that he had no physical or other problems in producing sounds. Incidentally, this imitating of a variety of sounds is something that was also done by Leslie, the late-talking girl Thelma Weeks wrote about.[22] It was also something that the great pianist Arthur Rubinstein did when he was a late-talking toddler.[23]

I told the parents that I expected Wally to begin talking when he was about three, which is when children like this usually begin to talk. The boy's father, an accountant, accepted my conclusion. But the mother remained worried, even though a pediatrician had also rejected the dire predictions about the child's never being able to talk. It is hard to blame the mother. After all, there were still all those others back in California saying dire things, and all that my conclusion promised was another year of silence to suffer through.

When this couple from California brought little Wally back for another visit at 34 months of age, he finally said his first word—*flower*—in my presence and with his mother looking on. The next day he said his second word, *turtle*, and later the same week, *fly*. When he was about three and a half, Wally's language development suddenly expanded explosively. When my speech-pathologist wife was visiting her own mother in California, she stopped by to see him, as she often does with late-talking children who live in places she happens to be traveling to. Wally was now four years old and speaking fluently in complete sentences.

We are able to follow some late-talking children over a longer period than most clinicians or researchers do. For example, there's a very bright, Einstein-syndrome boy we can call "Jack," who was not yet three years old when we first saw him in our clinical research program. We recently saw him again when he was almost ten, while this book was being written.

When we first saw Jack at 34 months, not only was he late in talking, his ability to understand spoken language was also below normal, more like that of a child only a year old. As noted in chapter 2, being below normal in understanding speech, as well as in developing the ability to speak, means having poorer prospects of developing normally—*on average.* Jack was among the exceptions. During his latest visit, I had to laugh when Jack's mother complained that he talks so much that now that she can't get him to keep quiet. He is constantly talking in general and asking questions in particular. In school, he is making good grades in most subjects.

Yet no one would have expected this if they believed the preschool's evaluation of him when he was not quite three years old. The school officials wanted to put him in a preschool class for children with autism, and their intelligence test—heavily weighted with tests of verbal skills—suggested that he was intellectually disabled.

Our evaluation of Jack when he was a toddler was very different from that of the school. What we found striking was that he was seeking social interactions, even when he couldn't talk, which is completely the opposite of children with autism. Little Jack would bring us toys to play with and point to the toys, as well as engaging in pretend play, which children with autism don't do.

When Jack entered kindergarten, he was slowly gaining ground on his peers, but he was still far behind in terms of speaking and listening. When the teacher and teacher's aides tried to force him to stay in "circle time," he threw mild tantrums and refused to stay put. Most parents are familiar with this ubiquitous preschool activity. Children are required to sit in a circle while the teacher reads a book or gives a lesson. But, like many late-talking children, he just couldn't learn by sitting still and listening. Because of this, the school recommended, and was insistent on, taking Jack out of the regular classroom and putting him in a segregated class for children with autism and intellectual disabilities. I participated in several conference calls to ensure that he was not removed from the regular class: I was able to show that their view of his low intelligence was based on biased testing and that he should not be removed.

Luckily, as noted earlier, special education law requires that a child be taught in a "least restrictive environment," so that the school personnel knew that our testing would not support a segregated autism and intellectual disability placement. Jack needed support, but he could (and did) learn in the regular kindergarten, which was the proper "least restrictive environment" for him.

To her credit, the speech pathologist working with Jack put aside her assumption that he had autism and began teaching him to speak and to understand. She spent many hours teaching him an understanding of words, word endings, and sentences. The progress was slow but steady, and each year Jack edged closer to the standards of his peers. By the time he was in second grade, it was clear that his latent visuospatial skills were superior: he learned to draw and could design sophisticated roads, houses, and shopping malls. He also learned to read and to comprehend what he was reading, so that by reading, he could understand any instructions he'd missed while listening.

Perhaps most importantly, Jack became very good at math. His mathematical skills have consistently been above grade level and even word problems, which many late-talking children have trouble with, are easy for him.

When the teachers could see that he was smart and capable of learning in a regular classroom, the calls to remove him stopped completely. Now, as he moves into fourth grade, all the big worries are gone: he does not have autism or intellectual disabilities and no one is trying to put him in a separate classroom. To be sure, there is still much he needs to learn. Jack's listening comprehension is nearing typical levels but is still a relative weakness. Also, his conversational skills are immature, and he misses indirect social cues. He does read facial expressions very well (unlike people with autism) and knows when he has made a faux pas after the fact, but he doesn't always know why.

Jack will have to be taught these things, and they are important. But, in the overall scheme of things, he is now past the time when mislabeling and incorrect placement and treatment will be pushed. His way forward will be much easier thanks to the persistence of his parents, the dedication of his speech pathologists, and the faith of the teachers that believed in him. Things would likely have been much different if his parents had not insisted that Jack's rights be protected so he could stay in the regular classroom and not be segregated into a classroom where he didn't belong and if teachers and his speech pathologist had not put in the long hours to help him learn.

Nevertheless, seven years after their false diagnosis, some people at the school are not prepared to abandon their dire conclusions. They recently told Jack's mother that he may have some form of Asperger syndrome—despite the fact that children with Asperger syndrome are not late in beginning to talk, while Jack was very late.[24] Even now, he is just reaching the normal range for speaking and understanding language, despite his high intelligence that has been demonstrated in school and on tests.

Children with the Einstein syndrome have encountered similar attitudes among teachers on both sides of the Atlantic. A classic example is a six-year-old boy in England I'll call "Simon." His mother wrote to me when he was three years old because nursery school[25] teachers there were pushing for him to get an "autism spectrum" label. Although his pediatrician had ruled out autism repeatedly, that did not stop the nursery school teachers from often suggesting that Simon was somewhere "on the spectrum." His mother told me the reason for this was that he didn't like to play with the other children at the school, and because he wouldn't follow the classroom routine. In addition, he wouldn't sit in a circle at "circle time" and listen to stories. In short, he would not do what they wanted him to do when they wanted him to do it— something he has in common with many other late-talking children.

Simon's mother wisely insisted that the teachers stick to teaching Simon, and leave the diagnosis to the pediatrician. Simon has a sister five years older. She talked and played with him every day and he was quite social with her, so his mother wasn't worried that he wouldn't play with other children in nursery school. She also told me that he could identify letters and numbers, and that the names of letters were some of his first words when he was three years old. At that age he could count. Later, at age four, he could add and subtract as well.

He could also, at the age of four, read words and then go find the appropriate object. For example, if the word *dog* was shown to him on a piece of paper, he would go outside and point to a dog. Similarly, if *chair* was written, he would sit down in a chair. If the word *shoes* was written, Simon would run upstairs to his closet to get shoes. His teachers claimed that this was "hyperlexia" and a sign of autism! But unlike Simon, children with hyperlexia do not understand the words they read.[26]

Simon started talking at age three, but unlike some other children with Einstein syndrome, he progressed slowly and was still saying only two- and three-word sentences at age four.

Like most late-talking children, Simon was not potty trained until age four. His mother told me that the school had been expressing concern about this since he was three and that the family tried to train him then, but he refused. Within a month of turning four, he suddenly, without any pressure from his family, became completely trained within a matter of weeks. This pattern is very common in late-talking children; they will often resist all efforts at potty training until they are ready and this is often not until the age of four.

In earlier generations, this really wasn't such a concern because the child was at home, but the recent push for early education and the mass enrollment of children in preschool at age three has resulted in parents and teachers wanting to train their children by that age, something many late-talking children resist.

When Simon turned five, there was a substantial "language burst," so that he began catching up. His mother told me that he was still behind, but the delay was much less noticeable. Because it was now time for primary school, she agreed to have him tested by a school psychologist. The psychologist also ruled out autism. By now, it was clear that Simon was quite precocious in both reading and math. The psychologist's testing showed that Simon could read as well as most nine-year-olds and had the mathematical ability of a ten-year-old. I tested him when he was five and a half and found that his IQ was in the gifted range.

By this time, Simon's talking and listening had caught up, so that he was only about six months behind in these areas and would not have qualified for any special education services. The teachers finally recognized that Simon was very smart and have recommended that he be put in the gifted class. But they still complain to his mother about his lack of cooperation in the classroom and the persistence of "red flags" socially because he still won't play with his peers at school.

The six-year-old Simon thinks like a nine- or ten-year-old, but talks and understands like a five-year-old. Mentally he does not have much in common with the six-year-olds in his class and linguistically he is behind. No wonder he would rather play with his ten-year-old sister and with eight- and nine-year-old friends.

Adults with the Einstein Syndrome

Three of the nuclear physicists involved in creating the first atomic bomb were late-talking children. It was Albert Einstein whose letter to President Franklin D. Roosevelt led to the creation of the Manhattan Project, and Edward Teller and Richard Feynman worked directly on that project.

Physics is not the only field in which late-talking children are found with the extraordinary mental ability that characterizes the Einstein syndrome. Mathematics is another. Julia Robinson (1919–1985) was the first woman to become president of the American Mathematical Society and the first female mathematician elected to the National Academy of Sciences. She had been a late-talking child. A famous mathematical prodigy from India named Ramanujan was another late-talking child who went on to great accomplishments.

Ramanujan was born in 1887. Like many bright, late-talking children, he showed an early aptitude for numbers. He mastered trigonometry by age 12 and won prizes in school for his mathematical ability. Also like many bright late-talking children, Ramanujan would not exert himself on subjects he found uninteresting. After leaving college, he continued his mathematical research on his own and, by 1912, had developed a number of new mathematical theorems. He sent samples of these theorems to Professor G. H. Hardy, a well-known mathematician at Trinity College, Cambridge University. This led to an invitation to attend Cambridge, where he eventually went on to become a Fellow of the Royal Society.

Although Ramanujan became ill and died prematurely at the age of 32, he left behind a large body of mathematical work, most of which has stood the test of time and proved useful in various applications, including crystallography and string theory. He was literally decades ahead of his time. However, in today's climate of opinion, someone with Ramanujan's combination of late talking, obsessive fascination with numbers, and lack of interest in nonmathematical schoolwork could be sidetracked into programs for people on the "autism spectrum."

Among economists who talked late were Richard Rosett, whose distinguished career included much scholarly work in mathematical economics, and Gary Becker, who also produced scholarly work in mathematical economics and won a Nobel Prize for it.

As children, many of these public figures exhibited traits found among late-talking children in general. Being strong-willed is one of these. Julia Robinson's stepmother had taught kindergarten and first grade and had a second daughter—so that she had dealt with many young children—but she called Julia the "stubbornest child she had ever known."[27]

As a child in elementary school, Albert Einstein fixated on the things that interested him and ignored the rest, raising the question of whether he had intellectual disabilities.[28] But, outside of school, Einstein's uncle—who was an engineer—introduced him to algebra and geometry, and the boy's progress in mathematics led him to the study of calculus while his classmates were studying decimals. Young Einstein's disinterest in other subjects did not sit well with his teachers, one of whom suggested he leave the school. Edward Teller was another late-talking child who was precocious in math, which did not endear him to his math teacher, who said: "So you are a genius, Teller? Well, I don't like geniuses."[29]

Distinguished economist Richard Rosett was another very bright late talker with problems in school. He was interested in learning and liked to read, but he was turned off by most of the material presented in his classes and became a behavior problem. He often took library books to school and read them when he was supposed to be doing assigned work. It was not until he reached the classes in geometry and trigonometry that Rosett became interested in schoolwork, and he quickly rose to the top of his class in these subjects. But the other assignments were so repugnant to him that he prevailed on his mother to let him drop out of school and sign a permission form so he could go into the navy—instead of staying in school.

After he returned to civilian life, Rosett fell in love with a woman who agreed to marry him only if he got a college education. In college, he found himself drawn to economics, and his outstanding work in that field led to an academic career in which his writings in mathematical economics were published in leading scholarly journals.[30] Had he not met—and wanted to marry—the particular woman that he did, he might have become just another of the many bright people turned off by school whose inborn talents are lost to themselves and society.

What You Can Do

Protecting children from an education system that all too often does not understand exceptionally bright late-talking children is one of the most difficult challenges facing parents. Be prepared to stick to your guns and insist your child be taught in the regular classroom—and not pushed into a separate autism classroom. Also be sure that teachers allow a bright late-talking child to work ahead in the subjects—such as math and science—while taking more time in verbally based subjects. No late-talking child should be forced to comply with "circle time" in preschool. Contrary to what you may be told, it is not a prerequisite to being able to learn in school later on.

Be prepared to nurture your child's intellectual gifts and preserve their natural curiosity and love of learning. Do not blindly accept reports of behavior problems. Investigate to determine the precise circumstances for the reports. On the one hand, schools have a right to expect reasonable behavior from their students. On the other hand, if the "behavior problems" are being caused by poor teaching practices insist on setting things right—or find another school that appreciates and values bright children.

6 Diagnosis and Dangers

With late-talking children in general, both the accuracy of the original diagnosis and the appropriateness of the treatment that follows are crucial. If you have questions or doubts about either, it is time to get a second or even a third opinion.

These second and third opinions should be completely *independent* of whoever gave the first opinion. That is, the other opinions should not be from the colleagues of whoever gave the first opinion, nor should the later opinions be from people who could be influenced by whoever gave the first opinion. The later opinions should also not be from someone who insists on knowing what the previous opinion was.

In my clinical work, I am willing to evaluate a child without knowing what anyone else's evaluation has been, but that is not always true of other practitioners. You may have to do some searching to find someone who is both professionally qualified and willing to give a completely independent evaluation. But the stakes are high enough that the extra effort will certainly be justified.

When a parent questions my diagnosis of their child, I don't try to convince them that I'm right, much less tell them that they're "in denial." I simply tell them my diagnosis and the reasons for it. When the facts force me to conclude that the child has some dire condition, I would be happy to be proved wrong, and I would hope that other practitioners would feel the same way. But all too often, parents tell me they have encountered condescension and have been accused of being in denial when daring to question the "experts." Far from being infallible, many practitioners in this uncertain field have not only been mistaken, but dangerously wrong in what they have said and done regarding late-talking children.

One of these children was a three-year-old boy brought to our clinical research program from Switzerland, where he was being treated because his language development was slow. The treatment he was receiving in Geneva was normally used to teach children with severe autism to speak.[1] My examination indicated that he did not have severe autism and was not a good candidate for this kind of treatment. In fact, he seemed like any number of late-talking children with specific language impairment I have examined or treated over the years: Unlike late-talking children with autism, he looks at other people when he speaks and what he says is reasonable, even though his spontaneous speech is immature, like that of a younger child, it is not robotic or deviant as is often seen in autism.

This little fellow is quite social when he is not being forced to talk. He speaks in one- or two-word phrases, while most children his age would be using at least three- or four-word phrases. But he shows no signs of having severe autism or intellectual disabilities. Nevertheless, for the year before he was brought to our clinical research program, he was treated in Switzerland using methods developed for children with autism. Because the latter children lack the usual motivation to speak, they must sometimes be prompted and given food as a reward to get them to talk.

So, the particular treatment to which the boy from Switzerland was subjected involves forcing a child to sit at a table while the clinician holds up various pictures, one at a time, and tells (prompts) him to repeat the name of whatever is in the picture. As described in one of the recommended treatments for autism in chapter 4, as each picture is presented, the clinician says "Say 'book'" or "Say 'mouse'"—or whatever is in the particular picture. When the child follows directions and imitates the words, the clinician loudly praises him, saying "Good boy!" or "Good talking!" and rewards him with a piece of candy, a cracker, or something else to eat. If he doesn't say the word, he doesn't get the reward and may be scolded for not trying hard enough.

Whatever the effectiveness of this technique for some children with autism, this little boy from Geneva is not autistic, and this treatment has disrupted his normal social development. Like many late-talking children, he doesn't like to imitate or follow commands. However, because he's socially motivated and wants to please, he has reluctantly gone along with this treatment. But what has been the net result?

In the wake of this training, this little Swiss boy seldom initiates conversations, but usually waits for an adult to speak first and then repeats what the adult says, even when he doesn't understand much of it. After looking at the adult's face, he looks at her hands. This may seem strange, and does look strange, but he has learned and been rewarded for naming pictures the adult points to, so he waits for her to speak before speaking himself— and he repeats what she just said, as he has been trained to do. Also, he gets the food from her hands, so it makes sense he's looking there instead of at her face after repeating what she said.

Think about how different this is from normal learning and normal conversation. In everyday life, food is not given to children as a reward for speaking. When talking, each participant speaks and the listener responds. The "reward" is sharing information and human interaction, not food. It's unusual and downright strange for any listener to repeat everything the speaker says, and in natural conversation, no one says: "Good talking!" and gives a piece of candy for imitating verbatim what was just said. Frankly, this technique is a last resort, even for teaching children with autism.[2]

After a year of this conditioning or programming in Switzerland in the name of autism "treatment," this little boy now smiles and waits for the adult to prompt him. This is very unnatural, even though very understandable in the wake of his training. The net result is that the whole normal conversational learning process has been disrupted. One of the characteristics of children with autism—repeating what others say, instead of expressing themselves—has been artificially induced in this child. Ironically, because he repeats what an adult says, an unwanted "side effect" of the treatment has been to make him appear "echolalic," which is a symptom of autism. He has been explicitly taught that unnaturally echoing adult speech gets rewarded with praise and food.

As if this clinical treatment was not bad enough, the child's mother was told to do similar things at home, repeating them numerous times every day, to the point where the little boy became bored, irritable, and uncooperative at home too. What this was doing to his perception of his mother, we will never know, but it is unlikely to have given him confidence in her love and acceptance.

Trying to undo this, I waited for him to speak first while I sat nearby, watching him play. Because I could see that he was social, I made no attempts to prompt him to speak. In this way, I was able to get him back into some simple spontaneous interactions, but it was tragic that his language delay had been made far worse by applying the wrong treatment. When I waited quietly, he quickly began to have simple conversations that were quite normal. His mother was amazed that he was so expressive and didn't need to be prompted to speak. In short, the "treatment" he previously received had actually interfered with his normal development.

Talking Without Restraint

This is not a treatment peculiar to Switzerland. It is used all across the United States. To facilitate such treatment when children won't cooperate, some misguided clinicians use a chair called a Rifton chair, complete with a restraining device to force the child to submit to the clinician's demands. This chair was originally created with restraints designed to allow people with severe orthopedic problems to sit up.[3] But it has been used instead to confine and control children in classes or treatment settings.

In 2007, a state education official in Wisconsin had to write a letter addressed to the Racine Unified School District regarding the use of Rifton chairs. She wrote: "The district was directed to stop using the Rifton chair with the belt, tray or any other type of restricting device, unless adaptive seating is needed pursuant to the child's individualized education program (IEP) because the child needs postural or stabilizing support due to an orthopedic impairment." The letter noted that when state officials visited a building where Rifton chairs were used, "it was confirmed that the Rifton chair with a belt was used inappropriately with certain students"—namely "for behavioral restraint, and for other inappropriate purposes such as a cue to begin working, a reminder to sit, help understand personal space, and acclimation to sitting."[4] Restraint of this kind should never be used as an "educational tool."

Please do not let anyone do this to your child in the name of teaching them to talk! You should also note that there is no such thing as generic "early intervention." Everything depends on what the specifics are. Early intervention is often a blessing, but could be a curse, depending on the specific intervention and the needs of a particular child. Tying children into chairs is just one of the misuses of "early intervention" that can do more harm than good, if it does any good at all. In a recent letter, the mother of a child in kindergarten in Tennessee asked my opinion of such practices:

I just got back from my son's IEP [individualized education plan] meeting. ... He's in kindergarten and is doing fairly well. He's never been a flight risk or aggressive in any way. They say he's one of the most loving little boys they ever met. But, the principal wants to write a "restraint plan" into his IEP. I got a little upset about this and she said it's just to give them permission to restrain him if they need to. I told her no way and they let it go. I would love to hear your opinion of this or if you've ever heard of a school asking to do this.

I had, of course, heard of such things, all too often, and wrote back:

The only time a child (or anyone) should be restrained is if the risk of injury is greater than the child's right to be free of restraint. This is not just my opinion, it is an accepted medical and human rights principle. So, DO NOT let anyone restrain your late-talking child unless they are about to go into the street, jump off a building, put their hand on a hot stove or otherwise injure themselves. ... I have seen too many late-talking children restrained against their will simply so they could be forced to do what the teacher wanted them to do. This is inhumane and inhuman. DO NOT ALLOW THIS TO BE DONE. ... I detest Rifton chairs when they are used as restraint (rather than as orthopedic support as they were intended).

Human fallibility guarantees that there will be incorrect diagnoses, especially in a field where the causes of delayed speech development are many and even internationally renowned scholars are still groping toward some better understanding of those causes. Outright cruelty such as what the mother described in her letter is just one of the dangers from incorrect diagnoses.

It is indeed deplorable that some preschools, schools, and clinics are using restraint as a routine part of intervention. Worse, it violates a child's basic human rights. When a family comes to the Vanderbilt University Speech and Language Clinic at the Bill Wilkerson Center, they will see a notice posted on the waiting room wall describing a patient's rights and responsibilities. This notice indicates that patients have a right to "be free from any restraint or seclusion unless needed for your care." This notice, which includes the federal government guidelines on medical restraint, is posted throughout the hospital and applies to *all patients* seen at the Vanderbilt Medical Center, not just late talkers coming to the speech clinic. Those guidelines state:

"§482.13(e) Standard: Restraint or seclusion. All patients have the right to be free from physical or mental abuse, and corporal punishment. All patients have the right to be free from restraint or seclusion, of any form, imposed as a means of coercion, discipline, convenience, or retaliation by staff. Restraint or seclusion may only be imposed to ensure the *immediate physical safety* of the patient, a staff member, or others and *must be discontinued at the earliest possible time.*"[5] [emphasis added]

Stated simply, patients should only be restrained when required for medical treatment. For example, when one of my own children needed stitches near his eye when he was about three (another child hit him with a swing on the playground), he was restrained using a "papoose board," which held his head still while the physician in the hospital emergency room gave him stitches. This is a reasonable use of restraint for medical care. And he was released from the "papoose board" immediately after the physician had finished the stitches.

Unfortunately, some clinics routinely restrain late-talking children as a part of their speech and language intervention or special education services. The belief seems to be that restraining a child using one of these devices somehow facilitates learning. That is, in order to get the toddler or preschooler to sit still so that treatment can be delivered, they are being strapped into chairs originally designed to provide orthopedic support, but which are instead being used as a restraint even when restraint is not medically necessary.

Make sure to specifically write into your child's educational or treatment plan that a Rifton chair or other form of restraint is *not* to be used. Be explicit and put it in writing. It's also essential to visit a classroom or clinic before enrolling your child. If Rifton chairs are being used for anything other than orthopedic support, you should seriously consider whether or not you want your child to attend that classroom.

Some clinicians have told me that restraining a child using a Rifton chair or other form of restraint is needed to help them learn. But there are no studies in the scientific literature to support this claim. On the other hand, there are hundreds of studies showing that late-talking children learn when *no* Rifton chair or other form of restraint is used.

For example, our own research on teaching children with disabilities how to talk has shown that many different goals, such as word learning, speech-intelligibility, and sentence use, can be taught[6] and we have *never* used a Rifton chair or other form of restraint during these studies. If the clinicians using restraint wish to argue that the Rifton chair or other restraining device is an essential part of treatment, they need to provide studies to back up this claim. At this time, *no such evidence exists*. Please be thorough in finding out whether restraint is being used as a part of treatment, and be explicit and proactive in guarding your child's rights to be free from restraint.

Dangers of a "Confirmatory" Diagnosis

By now, it should be clear that an inaccurate diagnosis for a late-talking child can lead to all sorts of problems. A misdiagnosis can result in treatment that doesn't meet your child's needs and which can even derail normal development. Worse, they could wind up being strapped to a chair and forced to talk! Because of this, one of the real dangers for any family with a late-talking child is that they will be evaluated by a clinician seeking to confirm *eligibility* for a preordained "problem," rather than seeking to determine whether the late talking is a symptom of a dire condition such as autism or intellectual disability. A clinician seeking to "confirm" the existence of autism spectrum "symptoms" in a late-talking child will inevitably "find" at least one or two "red flags"—especially in toddlers. A clinician seeking to confirm intellectual disability need only give a verbally based IQ test—or developmental checklist—in order to find one. Ask in advance what the clinician is testing for—and how the clinician will be testing your late-talking child.

As mentioned earlier in this book, a crucial recommendation for *all* late-talking children is a medical examination and an evaluation of overall mental development. And, all late-talking children should have their speaking and listening ability evaluated by a speech-language pathologist. But beware: A proper diagnosis *differentiates* among the various conditions associated with late talking. The diagnostic process should be conducted to indicate whether the late talking is a symptom of autism, intellectual disability, language disorder, specific language impairment, speech (pronunciation) disorder, and social communication disorder *or* simply a passing developmental phase with no long-asting problems. When a diagnosis is given, parents are encouraged to ask specifically how the clinician arrived at the diagnosis and whether other conditions were considered. For example, if an autism diagnosis is given, was an alternative diagnosis, such as social communication disorder considered and ruled out?

Parents should always ask whether the clinician believes it is possible for the late talking to be a stage rather than a symptom. After all, late talking is simply a developmental stage and not a sign of a serious long-lasting disability more than 60 percent of the time. A clinician should always describe to parents the specific factors that indicate their child has autism, intellectual disability, or another condition for which late talking is a symptom. Parents should always be encouraged to ask questions and should never be scolded for being in denial if they don't agree.

Consider that pervasive developmental disorders–not otherwise specified (PDD-NOS) and Asperger syndrome have been popular autism spectrum disorder (ASD) diagnoses that were ultimately dropped from the new autism diagnostic guidelines because these could not be reliably identified. But that doesn't stop some clinicians from pushing these labels and doesn't undo the heartache from the thousands upon thousands of unwarranted and unreliable diagnoses before these categories were dropped.

Also, when an assessment designed simply to *confirm* autism makes a child eligible for early intervention or other special services, this can create great confusion when a medical (differential) diagnosis indicates that a child does *not* have autism. Worse, because early intervention services are often focused on autism, the primary diagnostic responsibility for ASD rests often with autism specialists who are very well trained indeed in confirmatory diagnosis of autism and related ASD conditions, but who may have less training and experience in differential diagnosis of language disorder, social communication disorder, intellectual disabilities, or other conditions that share diagnostic features with ASD.

It is important to bear in mind that there are numerous educational, financial, and societal factors coalescing to support confirmatory diagnostic practices. In the United States, higher levels of treatment support are usually available for children made "eligible" for ASD services relative to other eligibility typologies such as language disorder or intellectual disabilities. And state guidelines often are fairly broad in terms of establishing ASD eligibility, so clinicians may have latitude in qualifying a child, even after a medical diagnosis has ruled ASD out. Similarly, there may be higher reimbursement rates for insurance coverage or guidelines for even getting insurance coverage at all requiring an ASD eligibility. Also, families that have an ASD diagnosis may be eligible for government assistance in the form of disability payments.

So long as the state guidelines are followed, this practice of confirming eligibility is completely legal and not unethical. Understandably, there can be a high motivation for a clinician to confirm an ASD, but parents should know whether a label is the result of a confirmatory diagnosis. Parents should ask point blank *before* the testing whether the clinician is only looking for autism to determine whether a child is eligible for services or is completing a differential diagnosis— and looking for something besides autism. Parents should also ask what percentage of the patients seen in a particular clinic come away with an autism diagnosis and whether any other conditions, such as social communication disorder or language disorder, are being diagnosed by that clinician or by that center. This can also happen with "apraxia," "sensory integration deficit," and/or "auditory processing disorder," so be sure to find out if just about every child walking in the clinic door comes away with same diagnosis.

Conducting confirmatory diagnoses of this nature can cause needless heartache and mistakenly place children in services designed for autism or other severe disabilities. For example, a preschooler we saw at the Bill Wilkerson Center (Vanderbilt University's speech clinic) had an older brother with classic autism. So, before coming to our clinic, the preschooler was evaluated by an ASD clinic as a sibling at high risk for autism. According to the parents, the evaluation completed by the autism specialist *confirmed* that this younger sibling should be placed on the autism spectrum. Of course, the parents were very distressed by this news; they knew firsthand from raising the older brother how difficult the road ahead would be.

But our own *differential* diagnosis indicated that this younger sibling actually had a moderate to severe *speech* disorder and did not have autism or even the broader ASD; he was having trouble pronouncing words, so people could not understand what he was saying. As is not uncommon in preschoolers, he would get upset when his parents and other people would not do what he wanted or bring what he was asking for. We enrolled him in speech intervention that did not include any intervention for ASD symptoms, and he reached normal functioning for speech in approximately 18 months, at age 4 ½.

To be fair, I did not assess this child until approximately six months after the ASD specialist had completed their evaluation, so it is certainly possible that there were salient autism symptoms present in that initial evaluation that were no longer present when I saw him. And, given the latitude in ASD eligibility, it is possible, and perhaps even likely, that he did indeed meet the state eligibility guidelines for ASD. But I should also note that this child did not receive intervention after the initial ASD diagnosis because there was a waiting list for receiving services. It is inarguably true that his pronunciation improved following speech treatment, and that *no* autism treatment was provided. Given this little boy's temperament and positive response to the speech treatment, which is quite different from the treatment used in autism programs, I believe that enrolling him in an autism intervention would have been a mistake.

Dangers of Inaccurate Diagnosis

There is another danger that may be encountered when seeking help—the fact that some ground-level practitioners act as if parents should not question their "expertise." I encountered such attitudes myself when my own son, who is a late talker like his father, was being evaluated for a preschool class.

Unfortunately, the test used by the school district personnel to evaluate him was a test heavily weighted with verbal material, which tends to give a very low score to a child whose problem is verbal. Based on that low score, these school district officials wanted to place my son in a class for children with "severe developmental delay"—in plain English, children with intellectual disabilities. When they said this, his mother began to cry, because as a speech pathologist who worked with children who have intellectual disabilities, she knew exactly what that phrase meant. But I did not believe them and said so, pointing out that his problem was with language and not with general intelligence. The evaluators literally rolled their eyes when I explained why I could not accept their evaluation and placement recommendations. Ironically, I had published a scientific paper on this topic, which, of course, none of them had read.[7]

When they set forth goals for my son to reach, based on his low score on a verbal test, I pointed out that he could already do many of the things they were setting up as goals for the future. But they clearly discounted everything I said, and even asked me in a condescending tone to bring a videotape to prove he could do the things I said he could do. They acted like know-it-alls, on something where my own clinical experience told me that nobody knows anything close to all. Sadly, far too many parents I have met in our clinical research program have reported this kind of condescension when asking questions about diagnosis or discussing the things their child does at home but did not do during the testing sessions.

After being told that my son could never learn in a regular classroom, my wife and I went around to various schools to look at the classes the school district officials had recommended for our son. Most were clearly classes for children whose disabilities were more general and much more severe than simply being late in talking and having some trouble understanding spoken language, so we refused these recommended placements. Eventually, however, we did find a particular class—for late-talking children and language comprehension difficulties, but not for children with more severe problems—and a particular teacher who seemed right for him. We put him in that class and he thrived there. His teacher, a speech pathologist specially trained to teach preschool classes for late-talking children, was absolutely fantastic and we will always be grateful that we found someone who believed that he could learn so much more than the "experts" predicted.

Incidentally, when we first received the diagnosis that so devastated my wife, the school officials tried to mitigate the damage by saying that at least we could spend the money we might otherwise have to put aside for his college expenses, *because he was never going to be able to go to college.* In fact, my son went on to graduate from college, so this prediction was as foolish as it was heartless. We did not, however, have to spend as much as we might otherwise, because an academic scholarship picked up a large part of his expenses. But the school officials' confident prediction, based on wholly inadequate evidence, is all too typical of what too many parents encounter from too many know-it-alls. I often worry how many children like my son never went to college because parents—and teachers—believed in mistaken proclamations from these "experts."

When you encounter people who dismiss whatever you say based on your direct observation of your own child, it's time to think about taking your child elsewhere. If you encounter such people in the public school system—as does happen— it's time to learn what your rights are under the law.

I have had to study federal laws on parents' rights in the public schools because I have been involved in many situations over the years, on behalf of my patients, where informing the public school system personnel that the parents have been made aware of their legal rights has been enough to get even stubborn bureaucrats to back down and let parents exercise the choices available to them under the law. That law, incidentally, is the federal Individuals with Disabilities Education Act, and there is an organization in Washington called the National Disability Rights Network[8] that can put you in touch with organizations in your vicinity to help you exercise those rights.

Fortunately, few public school officials are rigid and dogmatic. But you need to be able to fight back against those who are. My late-talking son had many wonderful teachers and clinicians when he was in public school, after we found the right program. And numerous families we have seen over the years also report very positive experiences and tell us about the heroic support provided by speech pathologists, special educators, behavior specialists, and classroom teachers in public schools. But you need to be able to fight back when anyone is rigid and dogmatic. You need to know what your legal rights are and to be willing to stand up for those rights, for the sake of your child. You don't have to blindly accept whatever label school psychologists, special educators, speech pathologists, classroom teacher or anyone else, chooses to put on your child, much less allow that label to become part of his or her permanent record that will follow them for years to come, causing teachers and others to treat them differently—and sometimes worse.

One late-talking boy who was four and a half years old came to our clinical research program from Minneapolis. When he was three, he had been diagnosed by his school as having "autism spectrum disorder." He was assigned to a classroom for children with severe autism. Fortunately, he was removed by his mother after only one day, because she saw that the children in the class had much more severe problems than her son had, so she knew it wasn't the right place for him.

Wisely, she sought an independent second opinion from a school psychologist, who diagnosed her son as having a receptive language disorder (difficulty understanding spoken language)—and ruled out autism. His mother then enrolled him in a regular daycare center. Today, he's doing well. I was pleased to confirm the psychologist's diagnosis. The little boy is now enrolled in a regular kindergarten. His reading is advanced and he won't be going through school, and perhaps through life, with an inaccurate label put on him. But only his mother's unwillingness to go along with the label initially proposed for him spared him this fate.

Cast of Characters

Diagnoses should never be presented as if they were indisputable truths that parents should not presume to question. But diagnoses, especially confirmatory diagnoses, don't come down from

Mt. Sinai on tablets of stone. They're created by fallible human beings in a variety of settings and roles, with very different levels of skill and experience, using very different procedures, and having very different incentives and agendas. Because the consequences of late talking can be far reaching, with many different diagnoses and treatments, the training and expertise of the clinicians encountered in seeking answers can be bewildering for parents. It's worth examining some of these roles and agendas.

Often the first professional a parent takes a late-talking child to is their *pediatrician* or *family physician*. This is usually a wise choice. People trained in medical science have been equipped with the knowledge to see through many of the fads and fetishes that other practitioners may promote. Pediatricians, neurologists, and psychiatrists, for example, are physicians. Other clinicians, such as psychologists, speech pathologists, occupational therapists, behavioral analysts, and special educators are trained in their specialties, but do not attend medical school.

If the child's delayed development of speech is due to some discernible medical condition—for instance, a genetic syndrome such as fragile X, seizures, or a tumor, for example—a physician is in a position to help. But there is often no obvious reason why many late-talking children don't have the usual pattern of speech development. All sorts of medical tests may show the child to be perfectly normal. As one physician said to me, "After we determine that the child is healthy, we don't know why they are not talking." At this point, the physician usually will recommend consulting a specialist.

But all sorts of people specialize in development and their levels of knowledge of speech and language problems vary enormously. Some physicians who specialize in treating infants and young children are pediatricians, and some pediatricians who specialize in developmental disabilities are called *developmental pediatricians*. A family physician or pediatrician may refer a child to a developmental pediatrician to check for developmental disabilities like Down syndrome, autism, and other conditions associated with late talking. This medical specialist may order genetic testing for Fragile X or other conditions for which late talking is a trait.

Neurologists are physicians who specialize in brain functions. They conduct medical tests for seizures, strokes, and other malfunctions of the brain. A primary care physician may also refer a late-talking child to a child psychiatrist, who is also a physician, as contrasted with a child psychologist, who is not. These specialists diagnose and treat conditions associated with late talking such as autism and ADHD. Then there are other physicians, called *otolaryngologists*, who specialize in ear, nose, and throat (ENT) conditions that may need to be examined when a child is late in talking, especially if there is a hearing problem.

Other clinicians often have specialized training in one or more aspects of child development and developmental disabilities. Although they have not attended medical school, most have graduate training in their specialty. An *audiologist* is a specialist who tests hearing. All late-talking children should be tested for hearing loss by an audiologist. You may be referred to this hearing specialist by a physician, or you may wish to contact one directly; but be sure to rule out hearing loss as a factor in late talking. *Speech-language pathologists*, also sometimes called speech therapists, are the clinicians parents most often encounter. A late-talking child should *always* be seen by a speech pathologist after a medical evaluation has been completed. Why? Because these nonmedical specialists are trained to evaluate a child's ability to talk, including speech development (pronunciation), how much a child understands, and whether the number and type of words said is reasonable for their age.

After all, the child is late *talking*, and a speech pathologist is *the* expert on talking.

As with many clinical disciplines, there are many highly skilled speech pathologists but also some who are less so. The speech pathologist who taught my son in preschool was excellent. In his book *Late-Talking Children*, Thomas Sowell reported that his own son had a very positive experience with a speech pathologist. But other children he investigated were not as fortunate.

The American Speech-Language-Hearing Association (asha .org) is located in Rockville, Maryland, and lists speech pathologists from all over the United States on its website. As with any profession, including medical doctors, it is important to check on the credentials and training of the speech pathologist doing an evaluation (or treatment). All should be trained in administering and interpreting tests of a child's speaking and listening (ability). And all should be trained to differentially diagnose speech (pronunciation) problems (including apraxia), language disorders, and social communication disorders. Some may have specialty training in autism and in behavior management, but not all will. You should also ask whether the speech pathologist has been trained to give an autism test.

Unfortunately, some speech pathologists seem to view late talking only through the lens of a particular diagnosis or treatment approach. For example, Marilyn Agin, who is trained both as a speech pathologist and as a pediatrician, highlights the role of apraxia in her book *The Late Talker*. Although a very few late-talking children do indeed have apraxia, most do not.[9]

Parents may also encounter speech pathologists who do not stick to accepted diagnoses and treatments, much like doctors who push chelation treatment for autism. For example, some speech pathologists may prescribe special tongue exercises, even though there is no evidence these help and there are credible reasons to believe these should not be used at all in late-talking children.[10] If a speech pathologist prescribes blowing exercises, tongue movement drills, "oral stimulation" and the like that do not directly teach speaking ability, you should find someone else to treat your child. But be forewarned, a survey conducted a few years ago showed that up to 85 percent of speech pathologists treating late-talking children use these techniques either as a primary or secondary drill.[11] Be sure to ask whether your clinician is using these techniques.

A few years ago, I was giving a lecture once to a local group of parents with children who have Down syndrome about why nonspeech oral-motor exercises—such as blowing bubbles—should not be used for speech disorders. Many children with Down syndrome have difficulty learning to talk, and nearly all are enrolled in speech therapy. One of the many things I love about talking to audiences with an interest in Down syndrome is that families often bring their children to the lectures. After my lecture, a 10-year-old girl with Down syndrome raised her hand and asked, "You mean no more bubbles?" I was pleased that she understood the point of my lecture and I said, "You are right. No more bubbles!"

Her parents came up afterwards and told me that the speech pathologist working with their daughter had been trying to get her to blow bubbles (and blow up balloons) for years, which their daughter simply couldn't do. So she was very frustrated and hated to go to speech therapy. On the other hand, the parents also said that this speech pathologist had taught their daughter to understand and read words, which they greatly appreciated and I applauded. I only wish that the speech pathologist would have used all of this child's precious therapy time working on these worthwhile goals rather than wasting some of that valuable time trying to get her to blow bubbles and blow up balloons.

In an ideal world, a competent speech pathologist will be a parent's partner and the child's "talking coach" as the child learns to speak. However, if you're unhappy about the way your child is being treated, don't hesitate to seek a different clinician or to get a second opinion.

Occupational therapist is a term derived from the role of clinicians who specialize in physically retraining people who have been injured, so that they can return to work. Occupational therapists are highly trained and skilled in teaching children to feed themselves, tie their shoes, dress themselves, use scissors, and write or draw. They enter the picture when a late-talking child is slow to develop fine motor coordination. We regularly refer such children to occupational therapists when they need assistance in acquiring these particular skills.

When occupational therapists treat late-talking children, their approach has often been to try to give the child physical abilities intended to make talking easier. But seldom, if ever, is a late-talking child's problem a lack of physical abilities. Nevertheless, occupational therapists may, for example, have the late-talker use swings or trampolines, or they may brush the child's arm or engage in other physical activities in the hope of helping the child talk. *None of these treatments have been shown to improve speaking ability.* Often a diagnosis of "sensory integration deficit" or "sensory processing deficit" may be used by occupational therapists or even some speech pathologists as a basis for these activities. But neither these diagnoses nor the treatments based on them have been validated by scientific evidence, and they are not recognized by the medical profession.[12]

My own study of sensory integration therapy shows that it usually includes fun, play based activities that the children enjoy. And the occupational therapists I meet, almost without exception are positive, friendly clinicians with a "can do" attitude. And some, such as Dr. Lucy Miller and Dr. Sarah Schoen at the STAR Center in Denver, Colorado, understand that sensory activities can be a means for setting up a positive communication environment for the child and are terrific clinicians. The problem comes when a clinician believes that wearing a weighted vest or brushing a child's arm (both widely used sensory procedures) are proper treatments for late talking. Never allow your late-talking child to be traumatized by well-meaning, but misguided therapists who force sensory exercise as a "cure" for sensory deficits.

Last year, as I was getting ready for a lecture, I noticed that one of the graduate students in the class was sobbing quietly at her desk. I asked her what was wrong, and she told me that during one of her practicum (clinical practice) lessons, an occupational therapist had forced a late-talking child to climb up on tables as a treatment for "gravitational insecurity." The poor little fellow was terrified and screamed the whole time. I assured the student clinician that "gravitational insecurity" is not an accepted diagnosis and that there is no evidence whatsoever that making a child climb on tables would help him learn to talk. Many occupational therapists I have worked with would *never* do this to a child, but it may happen. On a less traumatic note, some occupational therapists will recommend that a late-talking child have their arm "brushed" up to several hours a day, or even more. Again, some children do not like this, and there is no evidence that giving this "treatment" will help them learn to talk.

Child psychologists are another group of clinicians that parents of late-talking children may encounter. They do psychological testing such as IQ testing and achievement testing and diagnose intellectual disabilities, schizophrenia, ADHD and autism, among other conditions. *School psychologists* are trained to administer and interpret IQ and diagnostic tests and make recommendations for a given child's eligibility to be placed in special education programs.

Finally, because some late-talking children, such as those with autism, display behavior problems, a *behavior specialist* may come into the picture. These clinicians have a master's degree and are trained to treat disruptive behavior, such as tantrums, self-injury, hitting, biting, and running in the classroom. They are usually called "behavior analysts" or "behavior specialists." Most are very helpful, although some may rely heavily on verbal instructions—which may not work very well with late-talking children. Behavior analysts can be helpful in spotting—and solving—behavior problems.

Another problem is that as parents look for help for their late-talking children, they may encounter all sorts of people—and the knowledge of speech and language problems varies enormously among these clinicians. At one level, there are research scholars, usually professors at universities, who devote their lives to studying in great depth a wide range of problems and complex scientific evidence on the possible causes and cures of these problems. These scholars may have PhD or MD degrees or even an MD *and* a PhD, and they train students who will likewise earn these degrees and carry out their own research in the years ahead.

The findings of these research scholars appear in academic journals published around the world, so that what they learn can be widely distributed. Yet these findings are read almost exclusively by other scholars, who have similar scientific training and who can therefore understand what is said in the academic jargon of the profession—things like "cerebral lateralization" or "multivariate analysis"—and follow complex graphs and refer-ences to a previous scientific literature that most people outside these scholarly ranks have not read.

While these are a group of people with the widest and deepest knowledge of the complex issues involved, they are not neces-sarily the people that parents are likely to encounter when they seek professional help.

Unfortunately, the ground-level people with whom parents are likely to come in contact may not closely follow what is being discovered by the leading scholars in internationally known academic journals. In most cases, the kind of people who deal directly with parents and their late-talking children don't have the level of scientific training required, nor the time to keep up with that complex literature. In short, scholars and practitioners may operate in different worlds, not hermetically sealed off from one another, but almost.

What that means is that even when methods of diagnosis and treatment that have been thoroughly discredited by scientific research may nevertheless continue to be widely used by ground-level practitioners who deal directly with parents and children. In their own setting, these practitioners are interacting with par-ents who are often desperate and who are putting their faith in someone regarded as an "expert." It is, frankly, a setting in which some practitioners may recommend and, perhaps worse, firmly believe in questionable or even discredited practices. Fam-ilies may still find doctors giving chelation treatment for autism despite the FDA warnings or encounter clinicians who blame vaccines for autism, even in the face of overwhelming scientific evidence against these discredited theories. But these "experts" can be persuasive.

Although physicians are usually the most reliable of the clini-cians who examine or treat late-talking children, there are some physicians affiliated with particular programs committed to a particular approach, even when that approach has been discredited by research and repudiated by professional and scientific organizations. For example, physician-scientist Paul Offit notes: "By far the most extensive network of physicians offering alternative therapies for autism belongs to Defeat Autism Now (DAN), a group based in San Diego and part of the Autism Research Institute. Like Andrew Wakefield, DAN practitioners believe autism is caused by toxic substances that enter the body through a leaky gut. (Studies have failed to prove that children have leaky guts and brain damaging toxins have never been identified.)"[13]

Offit then adds: "About 300 DAN doctors practice in the United States. Although they often tout their treatments as harmless, they may not be. Vitamin B_6 injections can damage nerves, and excess Vitamin A can damage the liver and cause a build up of pressure on the brain. Many DAN doctors have been disciplined by their state medical boards for practicing medicine unethically or illegally, and several have had their medical licenses suspended or revoked. Two DAN doctors have been censured for injecting Hydrogen Peroxide intravenously."[14]

The FDA has not endorsed any vitamin or diet regimen for treating autism. A specific warning has been issued against chelation, a medical treatment that removes lead from the bloodstream, as a general treatment for autism. Both the National Institute of Medicine and the Centers for Disease Control have produced extensive scientific evidence arguing against vaccines as a cause of autism, and the prestigious The *British Medical Journal* has declared Wakefield's paper on the vaccine-autism link an outright fraud.[15] Yet parents may still encounter clinicians, even some with medical degrees, who promote treatments based on these discredited ideas.

Some may want nothing more than to get the respect and deference from parents that they don't get from scholars in this field. Some practitioners who are zealots for a particular approach may want nothing more than a captive audience of parents and a supply of children to serve as subjects to whom their pet notions can be applied. Others, quite simply, want money—and see desperate and trusting parents as a way to get it, by offering expensive treatments that in too many cases have already been discredited by scientific research.

Fortunately, there are also earnest and dedicated practitioners who simply want to help children, and who strive to do so to the best of their ability. Unfortunately, however, most parents have no way of separating one kind of practitioner from the other. But you can at least be aware that these differences exist, which means that you shouldn't simply turn your child over to a self-proclaimed "expert" and then blindly follow whatever that "expert" says, especially when common sense tells you something isn't right. For example, do not allow any "expert" to convince you that forcefully restraining your child in a Rifton chair is necessary to get them to talk.

Even earnest and dedicated clinicians may have a limited range of experience, despite having been treating late-talking children for years. That's because many clinical practitioners deal with children within a very narrow age range. Those who evaluate children for preschool, for example, may see many 3-year-olds but almost never any 10-year-olds, even if they spend 20 years in the profession. Those who evaluate slightly older children who are about to enter elementary school will likewise seldom have any experience that would tell them how these children turn out in adolescence, much less adulthood. These practitioners have little or no experience to draw on to tell them how many of the late-talking children they evaluate or treat are simply passing through a stage and how many have long-term disabilities for which the late talking is a symptom. While such practitioners may acquire a lot of experience with three-year-olds, for example, what they do not acquire is a chastening knowledge of how often their diagnoses have turned out to be wrong as the child's later development unfolded.

Those who tell parents that their child will never be able to go to college will seldom—if ever—have followed a child into the college-age years, in order to see if their predictions have proved true or false. Unfortunately, parents may encounter these kinds of clinical professionals and must be prepared to deal with them.

Among the few professionals likely to follow a given child from infancy into adolescence and beyond are pediatricians and other family physicians. That may be why so many pediatricians advise parents to be patient and cautious while awaiting speech development in a late-talking child, especially after the doctors have examined the child and found no medical problems that would delay speech development. An experienced pediatrician may have seen many late-talking children who eventually turned out fine.

But, pediatricians themselves do not usually diagnose or treat speech delays, but instead refer parents to speech pathologists, psychologists, or others who do. This means that although it is certainly possible that late-talking children can eventually grow out of this stage, some with and some without professional intervention, there are still some children for whom delayed speech development is a symptom of much more serious problems. Whether nonmedical specialists will attempt to separate the two kinds of late-talking children is the painful question.

Neither "wait and see" nor "early intervention" is appropriate for every late-talking child.[16] Everything depends on the particular child, and there is no one-size-fits-all advice—except from some crusaders for universal "early intervention" or a favorite therapy—for all late-talking children.

How can a parent know how reliable and responsible the clinicians are who treat their child? That's the huge question for which there's no easy answer. Some pediatricians may have referred enough late-talking children to enough clinicians over the years that they have acquired—from the parents' feedback—some sense of which clinicians are good and which are not.[17]

How can a parent eliminate the intermediaries and go straight to the leading scholars in the field to find out what their child's problem is and how to treat it? Unfortunately, that's rarely easy to do. Professors who are training graduate students working on their PhDs may have clinics where children are examined and studied, from the standpoint of how this process may advance the research agendas of the university scholars.

This is not usually a place where people can just walk in off the street and have their children diagnosed and treated. Moreover, even if the particular child's problem is being studied at that university, the person dealing directly with the parent and child is likely to be one of the professor's graduate students, rather than the professor himself or herself, though the professor may exercise varying degrees of supervision.

There are a very few places—Vanderbilt University being one—where the professor in charge directly diagnoses and treats late-talking children. I do that. So do other professors and clinicians at a few other places. But even in the program here at Vanderbilt where a professor does participate in diagnosis, I only see a small fraction of the hundreds of late-talking children that come through the clinic every year.

Professor Lynn Koegel of the University of California at Santa Barbara, for example, is an educational psychologist and speech pathologist whose work is widely recognized and whose writings on speech and language development have been translated into a number of other languages. She and Claire LeZebnik have written a popular, readable book titled *Overcoming Autism* that has many useful suggestions for late-talking children of all kinds, including those who don't have autism. As a clinician, Professor Koegel is not the kind of person who would strap children into chairs or do any of the other inhumane things some other clinicians do. She and her husband, Professor Robert Koegel, are codirectors of the Koegel Autism Research Center at the University of California, Santa Barbara.

Another scholar in this field who is also a clinician is Dr. James D. McDonald, who was a professor of speech and language pathology and development disabilities at Ohio State University for more than 20 years, before taking early retirement to develop the Communicating Partners Center in Columbus, Ohio. "Dr. Jim" is a no-nonsense clinician who diagnoses and treats late-talking children. His book *It Takes Two to Talk* is an excellent guide for parents, particularly those with late-talking children who aren't yet speaking or who are in the early stages of learning to talk, using single words or short phrases. Professor McDonald has worked with more than a thousand families, to enable them to help their own children's language development, and has trained more than 1,500 speech pathologists.

Professor Travis Thompson is a former colleague of mine at Vanderbilt University, who has also taught at the University of Kansas and the University of Minnesota. Dr. Thompson (a PhD) now heads an autism clinic in Maple Grove, Minnesota, a suburb of Minneapolis. However, he has specialized in the problems of late-talking children of all kinds, whether they are autistic or not. For late-talking children who are especially defiant or hurt themselves by banging their head or slapping themselves,

Dr. Thompson is a good listener, being both patient and understanding. He also has an extensive knowledge of medical conditions associated with late talking, especially with behavior
problems and genetic conditions, and so can be especially helpful with those kinds of questions.

Amy Wetherby, PhD, is a professor of pediatrics at Florida
State University. She is one of the world's leading authorities
on the treatment of autism and on improving communication
and social skills in late-talking preschool children of all kinds.
Her treatment approach has been adopted by schools in Florida
and several other states. In addition, Dr. Wetherby is a skilled
researcher and is a member of the Child Psychopathology and
Developmental Disabilities study section of the National Institutes of Health. The hallmark of her clinic is a genuine concern for the children and a strong commitment to empowering
families to help their children. She is also a strong adherent of
positive behavior support principles and treats every child and
family with compassion. Similarly, Dr. Wendy Stone is a professor at the University of Washington in Seattle. She performs
differential diagnosis of autism and has written a book on how
to diagnose autism.[18] And I know that she is very skilled at correctly identifying autism in preschoolers. Dr. Zachary Warren,
here at Vanderbilt, is the director of the Treatment and Research
Institute for Autism Spectrum Disorders (TRIAD) and is highly
skilled at differential diagnosis of autism. He has also published
a number of research articles on early diagnosis and early intervention in autism.

There are many outstanding scholars in this field, but how
many of them are accessible to parents, I don't know. What I
do know is there a waiting list of parents wanting me to diagnose or treat their late-talking children, and I suspect that other

academics in this field do too. Most parents may have to try to find some other kind of reliable clinician in their vicinity. In addition to seeking recommendations from a pediatrician, parents can find out from other parents of late-talking children what the clinicians they have consulted have been like.

Many parents who are part of our informal international network seek such information from others living nearby. While such parents are not experts, the information they supply may help a pediatrician or other physician to advise you on what looks promising and what does not. At the very least, physicians may be able to warn you against approaches that have been discredited by scientific research, but that continue to flourish anyway.

Doctors—and other parents of late-talking children—may be able to give you clues about the kinds of clinicians, or about specific clinicians, to approach or avoid. But you'll have to use your own careful judgment in a process that can be much like trying to find your way through a minefield. That process is examined in chapter 7.

7 Early Childhood Services

Parents of a late-talking child are understandably preoccupied with the fact that their child is not speaking, and these parents are usually greatly relieved when their child finally does begin to talk. But even after a late-talking child develops normal speech and goes through other developmental stages, that's not the end of the story. There are many additional obstacles to overcome, and overcoming them can be like trying to pick your way through a minefield.

Delayed speech and language development may turn out to be just a stage a child passes through, but the parents of a late-talking child still face a series of special problems over a period of years, and some of these problems do not go away, even after the child can speak and is otherwise normal or—in the case those with the Einstein syndrome—well above normal in intelligence. That's partly because late-talking children often have their own behavior patterns in other things besides speech development, and these patterns can persist long after the children have developed normal speech. Schools also have their own patterns, which may not always be compatible with those of late-talking children.

Developmental Stages

If we go back to square one, when the child is a toddler who is clearly behind schedule in beginning to speak, and then follow that child through school, we may get some sense of the landscape over which the child and the parents will travel—and of the minefields in that landscape.

The Earliest Years

The earliest and worst period of anxiety, and sometimes desperation, is after the time when a child usually begins to speak comes and goes without a word being spoken, followed by months and then years when the child is still not saying more than a few isolated words now and then.

The most obvious thing to do is to seek professional help. But that's just the first step in crossing a minefield (as described in chapter 6). Everything depends on *what* professional help, and from whom. My decades of experience with parents and with late-talking children, make it painfully clear to me that "help" sometimes turns out to be a waste of time and money or, in some cases, harmful. Among psychologists, speech pathologists, occupational therapists, special educators, and others, the range is from knowledgeable, intelligent, and dedicated people to well-intentioned but misinformed individuals, zealots, and outright charlatans. Most fall into the knowledgeable, intelligent, and dedicated category, but sadly, some do not.

So, no matter who you select to work with your late-talking child, don't park your common sense at the door. There are some people who take advantage of vulnerable parents' trust and desperation in order to push their own agendas, which can reflect a pet theory, an existing program, or simply a desire to make money. As mentioned in chapter 6, when you have doubts about the person evaluating or treating your child, that's the time to get a second or third *independent* opinion by someone who has no connection with whoever gave the first opinion.

Although physicians are usually the most reliable of the clinicians who examine or treat late-talking children, there are some physicians affiliated with particular programs committed to a particular approach, even when that approach has been discredited by research and repudiated by professional and scientific organizations.

Parents can get their late-talking child evaluated in the private sector or in some public institution, such as the local school district. No blanket statement can be made as to which is more reliable—and the danger of an unreliable diagnosis is considerable in either. Parents who can afford to pay for private practitioners to evaluate or treat their late-talking child have of course the widest range of options. However, there is also a considerable range of options available in the form of government-supported services, which may be provided either in the home or at schools by government personnel or private practitioners paid by the government. Services from state programs are available to toddlers, defined as children up to the age of three. These toddler services are usually provided in the home, rather than at school, and may include weekly home visits from early intervention clinicians, when these are called for. After a child turns three, publicly financed "preschool" services are available from a local school district.

The School Years

When a child reaches preschool age (defined as their third birthday), there is another range of services available from the speech pathologists, psychologists, and other personnel provided by the local school district. These may include one-on-one therapy or therapy provided to small groups of children enrolled in school or preschool. Broadly speaking, the hardest adjustments for a late-talking child are the early adjustments. In addition to the problems created by the child's limited ability to communicate in preschool, subsequent education classroom routines are often ill-suited to the late-talking child's way of learning and behaving.

The next stage in a child's progression is the transition from preschool to kindergarten. This transition looms large in the minds of many, if not most, parents. Fortunately, most late-talking children have begun speaking by the time kindergarten starts and many have caught up in most other ways, so that the late talking is no longer an important concern. However, many are still behind in speaking when they start kindergarten and are enrolled in special education at that time. This special education can take the form of a separate classroom, or it can be tutor assigned to help the late-talking child in a regular classroom. It might also be a placement in a regular classroom with one on one or small group "pull out" tutoring by a speech pathologist. Often, delayed speech development usually tends to become less and less of a problem with the passing years.

However much of a relief this may be to parents, they still need to monitor how well their child's education matches the kinds of learning and behavior patterns common to late-talking children even after they no longer have speech or language problems. When the child is being treated in a school setting, parents may need to give considerable attention and thought to both the therapy and the education provided. The quality and appropriateness of both can vary widely—as can the consequences for the child. In fact, either or both can continue to vary widely as the child grows older and passes through transitions from preschool to elementary school, from elementary school to middle school, and then on to high school.

Not only does the substance of the education change over the years, but so also does the way it's delivered, and some of these changes can make school a better—or worse—experience for a child who may have outgrown the late-talking stage but still has behavior patterns common among late-talking children.

Many are too immature to follow an unyielding schedule, others actively resist being forced to comply with arbitrary classroom rules, and many do not learn well in a highly structured, "sit still and listen" classroom setting. Many are "strong-willed," and may be a problem for the school, just as the school is a problem for them. The more rigid the school is, the more serious the problems can be. That's why parents of late-talking children need to be aware of these problems before they arise and take steps to prevent them.

Services and Options

At each point along the way, parents are faced with important decisions about the available services and other options for their late-talking child.

Placement Decisions

Where a child is placed can matter greatly and have long-term consequences for the child's development. After a child meets the state-mandated eligibility criteria for receiving special education services, the next decision is where these services will be delivered. The law stipulates that this placement decision should be made jointly by the parents and those who have evaluated the child. Even after the child has reached the stage of attending public schools under mandatory attendance laws, this is still a joint decision that cannot be carried out without the express written consent of the parents.

In the public schools, this joint decision is formalized in what is called an *individualized education plan* (IEP; also known as an "individual education program"). This is a contract between the family and the school system that provides the special education services. For toddlers below the age of three, the corresponding agreement is called an *individualized family service plan* (IFSP), which can provide services in the home, playing the role of an IEP for very young children who may not be attending any kind of school.

Contrary to what some parents report being told, there is often a range of placements that can be considered within a given school district. These include services in the child's home, contract services provided by a private speech pathologist or occupational therapist, individual sessions in a local school, and enrollment in preschool.

Preschool programs can be full day or half day, and some are two or three or even five days per week. Some preschools are "segregated " in that only children given a particular label, such as autism spectrum disorder, are included, whereas others are "blended" so that normally developing children and children with special education eligibility are combined in the same classroom.

Before agreeing to a particular placement, you should always visit the recommended preschool and talk to the principal and teacher. Also, rather than accepting the initial recommendation for placement if it doesn't seem to meet your child's needs, you should explore the entire range of possibilities. I strongly encourage you to visit a number of preschool classrooms and talk to potential teachers to determine whether your child would be a good fit for that particular classroom and for that teacher's style. That is what we did for our own late-talking son before enrolling him in preschool.

Among the things to consider when weighing placement decisions are the following:

• Are the other children in the class similar to yours?

• Are the teacher and teacher's aides positive and friendly toward the children?

• Are children strapped into chairs, forced to wear weighted vests, or subjected to other strange practices?

Avoid classrooms and clinicians who use techniques that don't meet your expectations of how your late-talking child should be taught or treated. Do not be misled by admonitions that highly structured classrooms are necessarily a good match for your child. Never forget that the school's agendas and goals may be very different from your own.

Some late-talking children do indeed benefit from a structured classroom, but many others do not and would do better in less rigid classroom environments. Also, the other children in the classroom should not be highly dissimilar to your child. For example, if your child's skills, outside of speech and language, are within the normal range, a classroom designed to teach children with general intellectual disabilities will not be a good match, because the information taught will be below your child's skill level.

Similarly, if your child is generally well behaved, I don't recommend placing him or her in a classroom for children with severe behavior problems. In general, it's best to place a late-talking child in a classroom with typically developing children and other late-talking children who are roughly similar in terms of their language and learning abilities. It's essential that the teacher and other school personnel believe the child can be taught using positive and enthusiastic teaching techniques that are flexible in meeting each child's individual strengths and weaknesses.

Having a positive teacher is the most important factor in the educational process. Meeting the teacher before making a decision is crucial.

Finally, if you learn of a good program in an adjacent school district, you can request an "out-of-district" placement, although good substantive reasons may be required before such a placement is approved. A number of families we work with have successfully found a good preschool program for their late-talking child in another district. This can be requested only if the preschools within the district or zone don't meet the child's needs and the IEP team agrees that the out-of-zone placement is warranted.

If no suitable placement is available, and you're in a position to do so, home schooling may be worth considering. In many cases, school personnel appear to have an implicit or even explicit belief that parents are somehow unqualified to teach their own children. Parents have reported to me that they're often actively discouraged from keeping their child at home until kindergarten. Somehow "early intervention" has come to be synonymous with enrollment in preschool in the minds of some educators, even though research shows that teaching a late-talking child at home can be a reasonable option.

A number of studies have shown that training parents to aid their child's development at home is a highly effective method of accelerating language development in late-talking children.[1] For example, studies in Canada and Australia have demonstrated that such parental training resulted in late-talking children achieving normal speech development at home[2]—soon enough for these children to be enrolled in a regular kindergarten class. Trained parents teaching a late-talking child at home can be an excellent solution, especially if the parents feel the placements available in the school system are not right for their child. Don't hesitate to ask about support services and parent training options at the IEP meeting if that is a possibility for your family.

Sometimes a placement recommended by school authorities seems good, or at least acceptable, but later experience can raise questions and doubts. Either the child becomes very unhappy after being put in a particular classroom or program, or the school may begin complaining to the parents about the child's misbehavior, even when that child had never been a behavior problem before. When this happens, the parents should *not* feel that they have to stick to the placement they had accepted before all this happened.

The law says that they do not. Moreover, early intervention and preschool services are not mandatory, so a parent can refuse these services and keep their child home if they wish. The parents are not obligated to continue in a program that is not helping their child or is making things worse. Some parents have even reported that their late-talking child has begun talking less than before after being placed in a class or program that was supposed to help their development.

Contrary to what some parents have been told by school personnel, a late-talking child does not need to be labeled "autistic" or "on the autism spectrum" to be eligible for services delivered either in the school or in the home. In most states, a number of categories of problems may make a child eligible to receive treatment through the public school system. Some states allow a generic "noncategorical" or "developmental delay" designation for toddlers and preschoolers. Although such noncategorical labels don't appear to have any long-term prejudicial impact on a child, a label like "developmentally delayed" may be viewed as indicating "intellectual disabilities"—*mental retardation*, in the blunt language that used to be common—in some states, though not in others.

If "developmental delay" is the general label school officials have recommended using to enable your child to receive special services, you should ask whether the educational team views your late-talking child as having general delays in development, as distinguished from simply being a late talker, or whether the team thinks the child has some form of intellectual disability. You want to avoid any dire label that is not warranted, for that label can follow your child for years to come.

It is important to keep in mind that, in nearly all states, a late-talking child is eligible for services under a simple "speech-language" label, so it isn't necessary to accept a dire and incorrect label that can create a lasting stigma.

Some parents report having been told by school officials that "more services" or "more appropriate services" would be available if a more severe eligibility label, such as "developmental delay," is used. *But the law says otherwise.* The 2004 reauthorization of the Individuals with Disabilities Education Act indicates that all services the IEP team deems necessary for a particular child are to be made available. In other words, a label such as "autism spectrum disorder" or "intellectual disability" is *not* required.

If a child is eligible under a state's speech-language disorders criteria and it is determined that a particular preschool program is necessary, that child would be eligible for placement in that same preschool program without having to be labeled autistic, developmentally delayed, or globally intellectually disabled. Stated simply, parents do not need to accept such designations in order to get access to a particular preschool program.

Always bear in mind that *early intervention and preschool are not mandatory*, so it is relatively simple for a family to walk away from services if things are not going well for their child in these programs.

Schools and Services

Local public schools are not only places where education goes on, they are also places where special services are available for children with special conditions, of which delayed speech development is just one. Although there are many excellent early intervention, preschool, and elementary school programs that meet the needs of late-talking children, it is also true that not all services will be what parents are looking for.

Enrolling a young child in preschool or kindergarten may involve testing or evaluation by the school district staff to determine what kind of class or program that child should be placed in. For a child requiring special placement, such as a child whose speech development lags behind that of other children the same age, this process can involve a formal meeting to create the individualized education plan or IEP geared to the needs of that child. This is part of a process that can be another minefield for parents to navigate through.

Despite the phrase *"individualized* education plan," schools often have a limited number of prepackaged programs that they try to steer children into. So it does happen that the particular program for a particular child has often been selected by the school officials *before* the first IEP meeting, even though parents are by law supposed to be part of the IEP team that develops a program. Moreover, even though federal law gives parents certain legal rights, documents spelling out these rights are sometimes shown to the parents for the first time only at the first IEP meeting when decisions are being made about the child's placement, before there is time to study those rights.

If a prepackaged program is sprung on you at the first IEP meeting—before you've had time to study the booklet detailing your rights—and you're being pressured to sign right then and there, it's time to simply walk out of that meeting. You're within your legal rights to stand up to the school officials. If nothing else, it will let them know you're not going to meekly allow yourself to be led around by the nose when your child's education and future are at stake. Many local organizations can advise parents on their rights in such situations, and the National Disability Rights Network (202-408-9514, http://www.ndrn.org) provides information to help you find these local organizations. It is possible to receive excellent services through the IEP process, as my wife and I did with our late-talking son, and in many cases things go quite smoothly. On the other hand, it is also possible that eligibility, placement, services, or goals may be misguided and a poor match for your child. Although the "I" in IEP refers to "individualized," it is nevertheless a fact that schools sometimes offer generic programs directed toward specific eligibility categories, not individuals—and push parents into these programs even when they are not a good fit for their late-talking child. Schools will often attempt to declare a child qualified to be in these existing generic programs or direct the parents to put the child in one of these programs. In today's special education programs at the preschool level that are oriented toward children with autism, this can mean substantial pressure to accept an autism label and placement in an autism special education program.

If your child does indeed have autism, this may be a reasonable path to follow. On the other hand, if your child does not have autism, the eligibility, placement, and services will likely not meet the child's needs. The combination of eligibility, placement, services, and goals should be *individualized* for your child's particular profile. If no existing program fits your child, the school is required by law to construct an individualized educational program that is in fact tailored to your child. A parent need not accept a generic program, and prepackaged programs are not all that a school has to offer under the law.

There are, of course, limitations: under the law a school is required only to provide a program that conveys an "educational benefit" to the child. Stated simply, the school is required to show that the child is learning. Although this is a relatively low standard to meet, I have been involved in cases where a child was placed in an incorrect classroom that did not demonstrate any educational benefit. In these cases, transferring the child to another program more suited to their needs significantly improved language development and related academic achievement, so that the previous placement was demonstrably wrong.

Individualized educational program (IEP) meetings can differ as much as people differ. When things go well, as they do in many cases, the assessment and IEP eligibility process are properly conducted, so that the parents and the school personnel agree on the label and on the placement for a late-talking child. However, there are also many other cases where there is disagreement. In these cases, parents have reported that substantial direct and indirect pressure was applied to them by school officials, in order to get them to agree to an eligibility label or a placement that was not in accord with the parents' own view of their child.

In some cases, parents have said that the premeeting interactions were positive, but then the atmosphere changed during the IEP meeting itself. For example, some parents report being reassured that their child had a relatively mild condition before the meeting began, but once the official meeting got underway, the parents were then pressured to accept a label of "severe developmental delay" or "autism spectrum disorder." Often, a large number of school personnel, including a psychologist, a speech pathologist, the school principal, a "special education" representative, and an occupational therapist, have shown up at the meeting and tried to push parents into accepting the consensus of the group, even when the parents disagreed with or were unsure about that consensus.

When this kind of ambush is sprung on parents at an IEP meeting, the parents should be prepared to suspend the meeting and request a follow-up meeting later, after they have had time to think about what has been said and what their options are. Parents need only tell the assembled ambush crew that the testing plan, eligibility, or placement was not what they expected, so that additional information, and additional time to digest it, are needed before they can approve the individualized educational program. Parents are within their legal rights to do this, and should never allow themselves to be rushed or pressured into signing something they do not agree with—and that can be part of their child's records for years to come.

Never sign an individualized educational placement plan unless and until you completely understand the eligibility and placement details and know who will be providing the services—and agree with all of these.

I have seen quite a number of cases where the family was unsure as to what label their child had been given in order to make them eligible for services. When I have reviewed the IEP with them and pointed out the eligibility criterion used, some parents have been shocked to learn that their child was listed as intellectually disabled or autistic. Always ask point blank what eligibility category is designated on the IEP.

Agendas, Tests, and Labels
You need to be aware that your agenda and the school officials' agenda may be quite different. What you want to know is whether there is something wrong with your child—and, if so,

what. But what the school officials want to know is if your child is legally eligible to be placed in one of their existing programs. If the school has some kind of "special education" program for children with problems ranging from dyslexia to autism, a late-talking child may become one of a variety of children sidetracked into such a program, in order to keep them out of a regular class for normal children.

If your late-talking child can be put into such a program by labeling him or her as autistic, then that may be done by school officials, *even if your child does not meet a medical definition of autism.* The law permits the school to use their own definition. I have seen this happen. Once when I accompanied parents and their late-talking child to school and objected that the child in question did not meet a medical definition of autism, I was told quite frankly that the school's own definition was being used. Fortunately, the label was changed after my objections in that particular case, but the policy was not changed. In other words, the next child in the same situation could be sidetracked into the school's special education program under a medically false "autistic" label—unless the child's parents objected sufficiently that school officials would find it prudent to avoid legal trouble or bad publicity.

The larger point in all this is that parents need to understand that what they are seeking from an evaluation of their child— namely, a reliable *diagnosis*—is not what the school is seeking, which is a *placement* decision for the child, among the school's existing programs, using criteria that may be quite different from those used in a clinical diagnosis following medical norms and practices.

Various tests may be used by school personnel to determine where the child should be placed, including an IQ test. What parents need to understand is that an IQ score on a given test is not an unquestionable, ultimate truth. Different IQ tests weight different abilities differently, and verbally weighted IQ tests often underestimate the intelligence of late-talking children, whose abilities tend to be analytical rather than verbal. In some cases, this underestimation of the child's abilities can even end up ranking a child of above-average intelligence as intellectually disabled. An IQ score on a given test is not something written in stone, though some people treat it as if it is the last word. Unfortunately, those people include both trusting parents and clinicians who take advantage of that trust to use the IQ test score to make their own diagnosis seem infallible—and any view to the contrary seem to be simply a sign of being "in denial."

Too many people with whom anxious parents deal in these early years of their child's life—whether clinicians in private practice or in public schools—will urge the parents to allow a particular label to be put on their child. This may be done to get the funds to pay for whatever treatment is prescribed, by tapping into money available from insurance companies or from government programs for children with autism, attention deficit hyperactivity disorder, or some other condition. But these labels do not vanish just because a child has long since outgrown the speech delays that caused such labels to be used.

It is not necessary to accept inaccurate diagnoses, and to let those inaccurate labels follow your child for years to come in order to qualify for services. There are federal laws mandating services for children with speech delays and other conditions that do not require parents to agree to permanently stigmatize their child. Whatever labels have been put on children during this period may continue to follow them in their school records or elsewhere. The word *confidential* is not something to rely on blindly. How many people will get to see those records in the years to come, and how many of them will talk with others about what they have seen, are things over which you have no control and of which you may have no knowledge when it happens.

Even when parents have managed to get an inaccurate label removed from their child's permanent school records, I have often advised them to transfer the child to a different school, if that can be done without creating too many problems. The stigma of the inaccurate label can continue to follow the child by word of mouth in the school where that label originated, even if the label is grossly false.

A late-talking little boy in Northern Virginia, for example, was tested by a school psychologist, and his IQ on the test was so low that it caused him to be put in a class for intellectually disabled children. As with my own son, this was a test in which verbal material was heavily weighted. When I tested this little boy from Virginia, using a different IQ test—one in which verbal material was not so heavily weighted—the same boy scored high enough to be put in a class for mentally gifted children.

Yet the school psychologist objected to the parents' efforts to remove the "intellectually disabled" label from the child's record, even after he was assigned to a class for gifted children. The school psychologist was simply not convinced that the other IQ test was more valid than the one he was using. At that time, there was no track record to show which test more accurately reflected the boy's mental ability. Subsequently this late-talking child did well in the class for gifted children—he was in fact a math whiz—and he is still doing well in classes for the gifted, now in the sixth grade in a school district with high academic standards. But that "intellectually disabled" label would still be part of his record and would have followed him for years to come, if we had not insisted that it be removed.

It is not unusual for a late-talking child to be eligible for more than one category. For example, a child could qualify as speech-language impaired *and* as autistic. In some cases, multiple eligibility will be helpful, such as when a child has behavior problems and learning disability. But, more often, parents should push for the eligibility that best meets their child's traits. If you disagree with an eligibility determination, but still want services, ask whether your late-talking child meets a different eligibility category. If the IEP team insists on an inaccurate eligibility in order for a child to get services, parents have the right to terminate the IEP process and simply send their child to regular school without an IEP. Thankfully, this rarely has to be done.

What You Can Do

After years of becoming all too familiar with the pitfalls of both private evaluations and evaluations by government institutions such as public schools, our clinical research program has put together a list of questions that you, as a parent, can ask anyone you're considering as an evaluator of your child *before* you make an appointment for the evaluation:[3]

1. What percentage of late talkers in your clinic are diagnosed as having autism or being on the autism spectrum? And, what percentage are diagnosed with intellectual disabilities? (Some clinicians put most late-talking children in one of these categories.)

2. Am I allowed to watch while you are testing my child?

3. Are you trying to establish eligibility for services? (That is very different from trying to diagnose your child, as explained earlier in this chapter.) If so, what eligibility will you be targeting? And will you be testing for more than one eligibility (such as

autism, speech and language, learning disability and/or intellectual disability)?

4. What tests will you be giving? Are you assessing IQ? How many autism tests will you be giving?

5. Will you be using a verbal test to assess IQ? (Verbal tests can greatly underestimate the intelligence of a late-talking child.)

6. How will you score an item if my child doesn't respond? (Counting nonresponses as wrong responses can likewise greatly underestimate the intelligence of the child.)

7. Who will you be sending the results to? (Adverse and incorrect labels can follow a child for years.)

If the clinician's response is "How dare you question my work?," that tells you more than any answer to these questions could tell you. Such a response is a clear sign that you should take your child elsewhere rather than entrusting his or her future to someone with this attitude.

8 Special Education Services: The Law versus the Practice

Federal law requires that special education services be delivered in the "least restrictive environment." This is a very important safeguard for parents of late-talking children who are seeking special education services for their child.

The presumption is that special education services should be delivered in the regular classroom to the greatest extent possible, given the particular circumstances of each child. For most late-talking children, this means going to the school in their district and being taught in a regular classroom with a typical range of students. However, there are some children with severe behavior disorders, severe autism, or severe intellectual disabilities, who simply cannot be included in a regular classroom. Fortunately, such cases are relatively rare.

Unfortunately, however, there appears to be substantial pressure from school officials, early on during preschool or during the transition to kindergarten, to segregate late-talking children into special classrooms, so that these children spend little or no time in regular classrooms or with typically developing children their own age.

Not long ago, I became involved in an IEP meeting in Texas because a late-talking child was recommended for a segregated classroom, and substantial pressure was put on the parents to accept this recommendation. During the meeting, the parents were reassured that the goal of these classrooms was to eventually "reintegrate" the child into a regular class at some unspecified time in the future.

At this point, I interrupted the meeting to ask the director of special education services to provide an estimate of how many children had been "reintegrated" into regular classes in that district over the past decade. After a period of silence, the director admitted that *no* children had been returned to the regular classroom after being placed in the segregated program. I then advised the parents to politely refuse this recommendation because I knew from treating their child that he should have been enrolled in a regular classroom. Subsequent events validated this advice, because that child is now in middle school and is at or above grade level in all subjects. Given the previous record in that district, the odds were very low that this would have happened if the original recommendation was agreed to.

Because so many parents do not know their rights under federal law, some educators may pressure them to go along with things the parents may have misgivings about, especially if it seems they have no choice if they want to get the services their child needs. But they do have choices, and they should not be reluctant to exercise those choices, nor intimidated by condescension from anyone.

Parents should bear in mind that the "least restrictive environment" requirement of the law is a powerful argument for refusing placement of their child in a segregated classroom. In nearly all cases, a late-talking child can and should be integrated with regular peers. The IEP should specify exactly where the child will be placed. Nor should parents allow themselves to be deceived by words or appearances. Sometimes schools attempt to meet the "least restrictive environment" requirement by "integrating" a late-talking child for such activities as lunch, physical education, recess, or art—but not for regular academic education.

A parent should be sure to get a clear and specific answer to the question of where their child will be taught and under what circumstances. If they subsequently learn that things were not done as they had expected, a new IEP meeting should be requested in writing and their child's placement modified to meet the "least restrictive environment" guidelines.

The actual placement—where a late-talking child is taught—can also vary widely. This can range from being completely in the regular classroom with that class teacher (which is called "inclusion" in special education parlance) to spending the entire day in a separate classroom completely segregated from the other students (which is called a "self contained" classroom). An infinite number of variations are possible in this range. The student may be taken to a "resource room," a separate classroom in which tutoring is provided one on one or in small groups. This may happen when a child is having trouble with a particular subject and goes to the resource room when the other students are getting taught that subject in class. In elementary school, my late-talking son went to a resource room for reading tutoring during the time when the other students in his regular classroom received reading instruction. This style of service is also called "pull out" and is usually limited to one or two academic subjects.

Another placement is called "mainstream," which means that the child spends most of their day in a segregated, self-contained classroom, but is "mainstreamed" for some subjects. Unfortunately, even though this mainstream time is supposed to be for academic instruction, I have often seen IEPs in which the mainstream time is just for physical education, lunch, and art.

I always advise parents to ask questions and be sure a late-talking child's placement options are crystal clear before signing off on the IEP. Some families find it helpful to have a class schedule, showing their child's proposed location by class period and academic subject, included in the IEP documents to ensure there is no misunderstanding.

Service Providers

After placement has been determined, who will actually teach the child or provide intervention services is then specified. In addition, the amount of time per week each service will be delivered is spelled out. For example, the IEP team may determine that a child is eligible for speech intervention. The program will then include a description of who will deliver the services and how often the child will receive them. The IEP for many late-talking children will designate a speech-language pathologist as a "related service." Many IEPs will include therapy sessions provided once or twice a week for 30 minutes (often in a small group) by a speech-language pathologist. Sometimes, the IEP will include "consultative/collaborative" service delivery in the classroom, with a speech-language pathologist explaining to a teacher how to adapt their lessons to the needs of the late-talking child. Although the 30 minutes once or twice a week seems to be a rather common recommendation, other services can be included as well. There is nothing magic about 30 minutes once or twice a week.

A number of families I know of received individual speech and language intervention for one hour, five days a week. Usually, a higher level of service requires evidence that this is needed to benefit the particular child's education. If the class or group includes children with differing speech and language needs, the child may not be gaining any educational benefit from this level of service. Some families have successfully negotiated higher levels of service by bringing data from previous interventions at higher intensity levels to show that their child can learn if sufficient support is provided.

Before signing an IEP, be sure you're clear on exactly how much time your child will spend in each recommended service, whether in a preschool classroom or in some individual treatment activity. You should also get specific information on whether your child will be placed in a segregated class—as opposed to a class for typical students—and if so, how much time they'll spend there. If the services specified in the IEP are not delivered, or the reality of placement differs in other ways from what was agreed to, you should immediately request another IEP meeting—in writing—and indicate that the school is out of compliance with the plan that was mutually agreed to.

It is the school district's responsibility to deliver the personnel and time agreed upon in the IEP, though it is not uncommon for them to fail to do so. Any deviations like this should be noted in writing by the parents and rectified by the school district.

Goals

After a late-talking child has been found eligible for services provided by the school district, and after the placement of that child and the amount and kinds of services have been agreed on, the actual goals to be sought from this process are written up as part of the IEP. Despite the fact that these are supposed to be individualized programs, a more or less generic set of goals are often specified, based on the results of standardized tests or on what existing programs are already doing for others, rather than on the particular child's own needs.

It is not uncommon for all children with a particular eligibility category, such as autism spectrum disorder, to have essentially the same goals specified. But parents need not accept this. Instead, they should take an active part in determining what goals are most important for their child. I am often amazed that parents are rarely asked what goals they think would be important for their child.

In the case of my own late-talking son, after my wife and I agreed on his placement, a generic set of goals was presented to us. I went through the list and informed the IEP team that approximately half the goals they set out for him to achieve had already been mastered. I will never forget the looks of disbelief I received. We were told that many parents have an "unrealistic" view of what their child can do. Other parents have told me that an IEP team suggested to them, as an IEP team suggested to us, that a videotape would be needed to document the child's skill!

We were given the impression that the IEP team would dictate the goals, but this is not the way the process should work under the law. Some time later, my son's teacher greeted me as I was picking him up from school. She had been present at the IEP meeting where I objected to the officials' goals for him. Now she indicated that my views had been vindicated, and that it was unusual for a parent to make such an accurate assessment of their child's abilities. The IEP team was unaware of my wife's and my professional work with late-talking children, and of the years of experience we brought to the meeting. Although most parents cannot be expected to have this kind of professional experience with late-talking children, nearly all have important insights to contribute to the process of setting goals that are truly individualized for a particular child.

It may seem strange that we didn't emphasize our background in the IEP meeting, but we both wanted to come to the process in our role as parents seeking their help, rather than authority figures. After we politely but firmly refused the placement in the "self-contained" classroom for children with intellectual disabilities, we wanted to give the team a lot of latitude in writing the goals. We asserted our rights in order to get the proper classroom and teacher and then turned the teaching over to her. Moreover, I had confidence in the teacher's ability to figure out his skills on her own, as she eventually did.

In fairness, it must be said that few school district personnel are dogmatic know-it-alls, though it is imperative that parents know how to deal with those who are. The parents we see in our clinical research program have given us many reports of excellent service from the schools. On the other hand, we also receive reports indicating that parental input has been minimized or even ignored, in the process of determining how a child will be educated or given special services.

Over the years, I have reviewed many IEPs for parents of late-talking children. Many have a large number of goals, covering many areas of child development. But problems can arise when instruction and services lack sufficient focus to promote the child's learning. This is especially a problem with children who may learn more slowly in some subjects than their peers and require relatively intensive and precise teaching to learn and to keep up with their classmates, even when these children are superior in learning other things. That's why one-size-fits-all programs are especially ill-suited to late-talking children.

In addition, some IEPs include goals that have nothing whatever to do with teaching children to talk or providing substantive instruction on content such as reading or math. For example, a number of IEPs include "sensory" goals such as getting children to put their hands in shaving cream, rice, or sand. Others include having them wear weighted vests or blankets to increase "focus" and to reduce "gravitational insecurity." Because parents have to sign off on the IEP, they have the right to delete goals that do not fit their child's needs. Many families have modified the IEP and excluded goals that do not focus on teaching their child how to talk. Also, do not hesitate to tell the team which goals should have the highest priority. One late-talking boy from Nashville would only eat a few foods, which the IEP team placed great focus—and high priority—on; but his parents were more concerned about his ability to speak. Because he was in no way malnourished, the IEP goals—and treatments—should have provided more time on talking and less (or none) on eating different kinds of foods.

Occasionally, even after the goals have been excluded from the IEP, parents have later learned that the classroom or clinician employs these strategies with their child anyway. Again, if this happens, an immediate IEP meeting should be requested in writing and the parents should insist that the excluded goals be immediately discontinued. In a few cases, when a classroom or clinician continues to use the inappropriate strategies, a family has been able to get a different placement for their child where the teacher and the support personnel will comply with the IEP.

Another problem with a plethora of goals is that few will actually be met and a relatively similar set of goals will be carried forward from one year to the next. For example, a number of children with autism I have seen over the years essentially made little or no educational progress under a generic set of IEP goals. However, after the goals were modified to fit the particular child's needs and development level, substantial learning in how to talk and in academic work was achieved. These cases are particularly heartrending because it has been painfully clear that much valuable learning time was wasted, when the child could have achieved far more if proper goals had been written up and adhered to from the outset.

One six-year-old boy whose autism was due to a genetic condition spoke virtually no words when I first saw him, even though he had had early intervention services in school. But within six months of focused intervention, he learned to use approximately 20 words. If proper teaching had been employed back in preschool, there is no doubt in my mind that he would have been using at least 10 times that many words by the time I first saw him. Valuable learning time had been squandered by the school in this case.

Instead of having a long list of disparate goals, the IEP team and the parents should make a much shorter list of half a dozen goals that are high priority and include these in the IEP. In cases where I have become involved in IEP meetings, I have often posed this question to parents and school personnel: "If you could teach this child one thing in the next three months, what would it be?" After they have answered this question, I have then asked what the next most important goal would be—and so on. The IEP has subsequently been modified to ensure that teaching and support services are directly focused on achieving these high-priority goals.

Teaching a late-talking child how to talk and how to use language in social situations should *always* be one of the high-priority goals because, after all, they are being seen first and foremost due to being behind in learning to talk. But some IEPs I have seen over the years include relatively few goals associated with teaching a child how to talk, even when that's the whole reason for the special placement and special services. Often, school officials seem to operate on an implicit assumption that general enrichment will suffice, or that peripheral activities such as "joint compression," "brushing," "sitting attentively," "paying attention," or "sorting colors" will teach a child to talk.

Such diffuse IEP goals should be modified so that *teaching vocabulary, using longer sentences, asking questions and understanding questions that others ask,* as well as *understanding words* in general are the focused goals toward which teaching and support services are directed. In addition, teaching a child to use the newly learned language skills in social situations should be targeted. In some cases, an assumption apparently exists that teaching a child to name pictures or to ask a rote set of questions during drill will transfer to other children and to conversations. But this is not automatically true. The goals and learning should be measured, not only in a therapy room but also in the classroom and at home and with other child as well as adults. The point here is that the goals should be *functional* and taught to be used in the appropriate social context.

When working with parents, we also often encounter IEP goals that are more demanding than even typical children at that age level could handle. For example, I have seen IEP goals requiring three-year-olds to use pronouns like *you, he, she, his,* and *hers* correctly even though many three-year-olds make mistakes when using these forms.[1] I have also seen goals that require late-talking preschoolers to listen to, remember, and organize complicated stories, even though few typically developing children could do this correctly. It makes no sense for a late-talking child to be expected to say and understand things that typical children at the same age can't do.[2]

Finally, it may be necessary to be specific about what teaching activities should *not* be employed. Unfortunately, as described in chapter 6, it is not uncommon in some clinics and preschools to use undue restraint with a late talker in the mistaken belief that such restraint is required for learning. It is perfectly fine to expect a late-talking child to stay in the classroom and not run away or leave without permission. This running away is termed *elopement*, which I find an odd way of describing a child who runs away. In any event, it is perfectly reasonable for a teacher to place an aide in front of the door so the child can't escape. On the other hand, it is not reasonable for an aide to physically restrain the child in order to keep him or her in circle time. Nor is it reasonable to belt them into a special chair, hold them face down on a beanbag, or pick them up and hold them against a wall. Yet all of these things have been done, at one time or other, to late-talking children.

Parents should calmly ask whether any kind of restraint is used in the school district, and if so, what types. Any objectionable restraint should be specifically excluded in writing in the IEP. In particular, I recommend that it be spelled out in the IEP that no undue restraint, using special chairs such as Rifton chairs, is permitted. Also, I highly recommend that it be clear that the school is not allowed to put the child in a "time-out" room. Some schools use a form of isolation in a small dark room as a form of punishment.[3] Unfortunately, a number of classrooms employ these and other inhumane force tactics with late-talking children. Most do not, but it is best to take no chances by inserting these prohibitions into the IEP in writing.

In summary, many families report receiving excellent services from the schools. On the other hand, others describe being pressured into accepting labels they don't agree with, having their child placed in classrooms they don't believe fit their child, or having IEP goals that don't address their child's needs. Parents of late-talking children should enter the process with a firm knowledge of their rights and a clear view of what they want for their child. If things go awry, parents should be prepared to shape the process to the benefit of their child and, if necessary, walk away from the process—and retain a professional advocate or even a special education attorney if needed.

Always bear in mind that your child needs you to be vigilant, and that—because they can't speak for themselves—it's all the more important for you to stand up for them.

Earlier chapters have emphasized the entry of a late-talking child into the school system because that's where both the child and the parents are most vulnerable. In other words, it's where there are the most mines in the minefield. But most of a child's educational years come later, and that scene has its own special problems and opportunities.

Late-Talking Children's Learning Patterns

My observations over decades have convinced me that late-talking children usually have their own special behavior patterns—and that these patterns continue, even after their speech and language develop. I see these patterns in myself, as well as in the children I treat; and follow-up studies of late-talking children support this view.[1] Unfortunately, too many schools have a fixed way of teaching, and their one-size-fits-all approach doesn't work well with some children, including those whose IQs are very high or low, or who have the kinds of behavior patterns typical of late-talking children, even after speech is no longer a problem for them.

For children with the Einstein syndrome, there is a whole set of additional problems found in high-IQ children in general, who are attending schools rigidly geared to other children. Many studies have found special problems that unusually bright children have in the public schools, regardless of whether they might have talked late. An excellent book on education practices for gifted children is *A Nation Deceived: How Schools Hold Back America's Brightest Students* by Nicholas Colangelo, Susan Assoiline, and Miraca Gross, all PhDs.

Many of the problems revolve around the boredom and frustration of these very bright children, and the behavior problems that often arise from that boredom and frustration. The school's insistence that everyone study the same things in lockstep means that bright children often have to endure mind-numbing repetition of material they mastered earlier—perhaps even years earlier.

Unfortunately, these problems can be at their worst in the early school years. The great, hidden danger is that they will turn the child against school early on, with lasting negative consequences for his or her attitude toward learning. In a world where education increasingly influences one's fate in life, making school a tedious and frustrating experience can create a large and lasting problem.

The principle on which most preschool and early elementary school classrooms are run can often be summed up as "be quiet, sit still, and listen." Many late-talking children are fine with the "be quiet" part of this formula, but the "sit still" and the "listen" part can lead to trouble. Most of these children tend to learn by watching and then doing, rather than by listening. In fact, talking at them is usually the least effective way of teaching a late-talking child anything. Unfortunately, early intervention services are often designed to force children to adapt to a "sit still and listen" process. The net result is that classes or treatment services based on that process could turn out to be ineffective or even counterproductive.

Most late-talking children learn much better in "show and tell" mode than they do in "sit still and listen" mode. That is, it is often better to teach late-talking children by first showing them and then explaining, using plain language. Because of this, early intervention and preschool placements designed to shape a child into accepting a "sit still and listen" learning style can include intervention goals and procedures not well suited to teaching a late talker how to talk or how to learn other things.

Some schools do have early intervention and preschool programs that fit a late-talking child's individual learning style, so it is worthwhile for parents to explore various options that may be available locally. In general, late-talking children are much more interested in exploring and learning things in their own way and at their own pace. As a result, preschool and the primary grades are often very difficult for such children, and this stage can also be a source of anxiety for teachers and parents.

The good news is that most late-talking children do much better in high school and college, when they are permitted to learn more of the educational content on their own by reading or by experimenting, rather than having to follow the process prescribed by the teacher. So it is not surprising that academic performance often improves as a late-talking child enters high school. Educational performance is often best of all in college, where the means of acquiring knowledge are pretty much left up to the individual, and the students now have more freedom to select their own plans of study, so that fields such as science, mathematics, and engineering may be preferred over courses that require a "be quiet, sit still, and listen" mode.

Because many late-talking children are poor learners in the teaching styles used in preschool and elementary school, parents may be told, as we were, that their child has attention deficit hyperactivity disorder (ADHD) or is unintelligent and may not be able to graduate from high school, much less college. Parents may wonder how to navigate these early years, so that the inherent curiosity and love of learning that are an integral part of most late-talking children's mindset won't be undermined as they get older, lessening the likelihood that their inherent intelligence will translate into better academic performance.

Schools' Teaching Patterns

The overwhelming majority of late-talking children are stronger in visual and spatial learning abilities than in their speaking and listening abilities.[2] There are some exceptions, of course, but for most, their strengths tend to be in mathematical reasoning, visual symbol systems such as numbers and letters, graphic abilities, and science—all of which may become important assets later in their educational careers. This suggests that an alternative approach to education may be more effective for late-talking children. But too many schools lack the flexibility to do this. Worse, many preschool and early elementary school teachers are not strong in math and science themselves and are ill equipped to foster these subjects in their students, which may put a late-talking child at an even further disadvantage in these early grades.[3]

When searching for early intervention or preschool services, parents should seek teachers, clinicians, and classrooms that are active and fun. There should *not* be an emphasis on a child sitting still while long periods of verbal instruction are delivered. Nor should there be an overemphasis on completing worksheets while sitting at a desk or table. Instead, look for classrooms that have visually engaging toys and materials. Children should be allowed to follow their interests, with the teacher or teacher's aide reacting to these interests rather than constantly prompting the students to sit still and listen to the teacher.

Similarly, early intervention should focus on educating parents to facilitate talking at home. Direct services should be child-led and play-based, and they should be designed to teach key things that facilitate the child's language development. If the focus of training is on getting the child to comply with arbitrary rules or fashions, the classroom and the teacher are probably not a good match for a late-talking child. Bear in mind that many brilliant students never participated in circle time or other arbitrary practices.

Teaching Content versus Compliance

There is a fundamental difference between focusing on teaching educational content—that is, knowledge—and teaching compliance with rigid rules. Teaching content means teaching reading, mathematics, and science in a way that increases a student's interest in these subjects. Unfortunately, too often the primary focus of early education is on immediate compliance with the teacher's verbal directives—in other words, on training a child to comply with the process of "be quiet, sit still, and listen." This approach is a mismatch for late-talking children for at least two reasons. First, many are strong-willed, so that attempting to force anything on them is an invitation to start a conflict that the late-talking child will go to great lengths to win. Second, many preschool children, late talking or not, are not very good at sitting still or listening, and so may not learn from what the teacher is saying. Adopting a compliance-for-compliance's-sake method of teaching is unlikely to be successful, and in fact may be harmful to a late-talking child.

There seems to be a widely held belief that, in order for students to learn, they must first be conditioned to engage in a learning process that primarily consists of listening to teacher instructions and teacher directives. Activities such as lining up on command, being quiet, sitting still, and listening, as well as transitioning smoothly from one learning center to another on time, are often the focus of teaching in preschool and kindergarten. But my experience over the years has been that a focus on compliance rather than on learning has seldom been successful with late-talking children.

In earlier years, before kindergarten and more recently preschool became so widespread, students entering the first grade went directly to sitting at their desks, rather than going through a preliminary "circle time" stage. Yet there is no evidence that missing this allegedly crucial "circle time" had any detrimental effect on learning. Did Aristotle have circle time as a small child? It seems even less likely that Einstein—a late talker—would have done better, or as well, if circle time had been forced on him at all costs. Clearly, participating in circle time is not a prerequisite for learning.

For a parent, the first task when encountering the education system in which their child is to be placed is to determine what knowledge is expected at the end of each learning block—and also to determine whether that knowledge is the teacher's main goal, rather than compliance with nonessential activities such as circle time. Teachers should explicitly inform the parents what knowledge the child is expected to acquire. For example, are they expected to know their letters and numbers? Are they expected to know the days of the week, the months of the year, and the seasons? The parents can then work with the teacher to ensure that their late-talking child knows the educational content they are expected to master.

Goals such as "will sit still" and "make transitions on command" are not worthwhile educational goals just because they are insisted on by some teachers.

Parents should seek teachers whose primary focus is teaching their child educational material, and who understand that there will be individual differences in the way their pupils learn. Teachers who insist that everyone do it "my way or the highway" should be avoided. Effective teachers are excited about helping a child learn. Conversations with these teachers show that they're focused on a child's strengths rather than on telling the parents why their child can't learn. When you hear a laundry list of "red flags" and excuses about why your late-talking child can't learn, find another teacher.

One of the rigidities often found in today's public schools is the notion that academic subjects such as math, reading, and science should be taught "at grade level," so that instructions are provided at the "average" skill level across these subjects for the students in a particular grade. But late-talking children may not be "at grade level," in any subject. Instead, they are often above grade level in some subjects and below grade level in others. Being stronger in visual-spatial reasoning, as many late-talking children are, can lead to faster and deeper learning in mathematics and science. But being weaker in learning by listening can mean having more difficulty and lower performance in the social sciences, language arts, and reading comprehension. My late-talking son was below grade level in reading, but above grade level in math and science. Thankfully, his elementary school teacher allowed him to work ahead in math and science and was patient with reading.

A school that sticks rigidly to teaching strictly at "grade level" in all subjects is not a good match for most late-talking children. Because many of these children are not interested in paying attention to lessons and content they have already learned, such a mismatch can result in reports of "problem" behaviors in otherwise well-behaved children. If teachers say that such a student has ADHD, parents need to seek an independent professional opinion about whether the child actually has that disorder. A diagnosis of ADHD is not within the competence of teachers or most other school personnel, though blaming the child is easier than reexamining their own rigidities. ADHD should never be diagnosed solely based on what a child does in school—or at the insistence of a teacher.

Too many educators see the child as the problem and medication as the answer. Reconsidering their policies—and, frankly, compulsions and rigidities—is apparently out of the question for them. They are willing to risk the side effects of medication instead.

My own experience as a late-talking child may be relevant here. I was often restless and bored in school, when the class was being taught things I already knew. Fortunately, one teacher allowed me to sit quietly in the back of the room and read material from other classes. But few teachers have such flexibility.

The overwhelming majority of late-talking children enjoy learning and are often voracious knowledge seekers. If left to their own devices, they can be counted on to learn, even if the knowledge is self-taught. For example, many late-talking children teach themselves to read and many began learning math on their own. Parents and teachers must work together to craft individualized lessons that meet the uneven educational profile of many late-talking children—and avoid forcing them to "pay attention" when the educational content is below (or too far above) their current knowledge level.

The Role of Parents

One of the real tragedies in the field of educating late-talking children is the implicit or explicit assumption that parents are somehow part of the problem and are grossly unqualified to teach their own late-talking child. Well-meaning but often misguided relatives, neighbors, and teachers may strongly suggest that a late-talking child requires preschool as an essential treatment. Children with classic autism—or intellectual disabilities—certainly present unique challenges and have technical special education requirements that parents may not be able to cope with at home, so that special services—and a special classroom—may be required. But the overwhelming majority of late-talking children don't have autism or intellectual disabilities, and they may be better off at home in the care of their parents.

Parents are often the best teachers for their children, particularly as toddlers and preschoolers. For example, because one key predictor of learning is the number of meaningful responses children receive from an adult, in most cases the home is a much better source of these responses. A large study in England showed that a home program with parents teaching their preschool-age late-talking child was a very effective early intervention.[4] After all, which environment is more likely to be responsive to children's initiations and interests: a daycare center or preschool with eight or more children that is staffed by individuals who can't love the late-talking children nearly as much as their parents—or a home environment with a much lower "student-to-teacher" ratio (at home, the "teacher" is the parent) and an interaction partner (the parent) who knows the child, loves the child, and has myriad opportunities to interact during daily routines?

For parents who for economic or other reasons wish to enroll their child in preschool, this information is not intended to induce guilt. Preschools, if properly conducted, are not detrimental to a late-talking child and many families report positive experiences with them. On the other hand, many families who are in a position to keep their child at home instead send them to a "special" preschool that the child doesn't like and that the parents may not like either, in the mistaken belief that this is somehow necessary for the child to learn. In many cases, the home environment could be better for that child.

On the other hand, if a late-talking child requires extensive intervention or truly has autism or intellectual disabilities, a preschool can often be important in supplementing home interaction with intervention support from skilled clinicians and special education teachers. Moreover, these children will usually learn more slowly in preschool and elementary school years—and often beyond—so that a combination of teaching and intervention support can be very helpful. For example, children with Down syndrome, with rare exceptions, not only talk late but also generally learn more slowly. However, that is not the situation with most late-talking children.

Another key point is that if a parent tries a preschool and finds that it is not a good match for their late-talking child, they should not be made to feel that it is detrimental to discontinue the preschool services. For instance, although most late-talking children don't have autism, schools may nevertheless place them in preschool programs oriented toward children with that condition.

Children with autism have low or no motivation to engage in social interaction with anyone (including parents) and therefore often require external motivation to get them to interact. As an example, a first step in teaching a child with autism to communicate can be to determine preferred food items and to teach them to name these foods as a form of requesting. For late-talking children without autism, this approach can actually decrease their motivation to talk because they already have an interest in social interaction, and forcing them to imitate may not have the intended result.

Many children with autism also have severe behavior problems and require fairly structured and special behavioral intervention programs. But the behavior management techniques employed for children with autism may not be right for a late-talking child who is not autistic. Because of this, many aspects of a preschool classroom set up properly to educate a child with autism may not provide a good environment for a child who is simply late in beginning to talk. If a parent discovers that the preschool the school district has recommended, or that the preschool their late-talking child is enrolled in, is not a good match for their child, there should be no hesitation or remorse in refusing the placement recommendation or even withdrawing the child from that preschool.

Be forewarned that there may be a high degree of direct or indirect pressure to accept the recommended placement or to continue enrollment in the preschool as being "in the best interests" of the child. But parents should trust their own instincts and common sense as to whether a particular classroom is a good place for their child. Never be browbeaten into keeping a late-talking child in a school that is not meeting your child's needs.

An educational minefield that must be navigated all too often is that some schools may not be completely forthcoming in their recommendations. Recently, a three-and-a-half-year-old boy from Illinois visited our clinical research program and his parents brought the school report. They were shocked to learn that his preschool had diagnosed him as intellectually disabled and autistic and had specifically excluded him from attending class with typical children.

When the parents visited the preschool, they saw that the other children had Down syndrome or severe autism and were not like their son at all. But when they questioned whether this was the right place for their child, the special education team insisted this was the only classroom available and was where he needed to be.

Our testing showed that his intelligence was actually above average, and he had already taught himself to read words and do simple math problems. He had little in common with the other children in this class and the lessons were far below his ability level. The school's own learning data showed that he was learning far more quickly than they had predicted, but this didn't stop them from insisting that he stay in that classroom.

The report also deceived the parents regarding the use of restraint and Rifton chairs, saying that "by signing [this report] the parents give permission for a chair with a seat belt to be used as a positive behavior support for sitting still." The parents were understandably upset when I explained the ways that Rifton chairs were often used to restrain children against their will and that the use of these chairs had been banned in Racine, Wisconsin, as a restraint method. They had no idea that their signature was authorizing this kind of abusive treatment for their child! I am pleased to report that the parents withdrew their child from this preschool after visiting us and are now teaching him at home.

What You Can Do

Entering preschool or kindergarten when a child isn't talking or has only recently begun to catch up is understandably, and predictably, a difficult process. But families I work with are often surprised that problems in education continue through elementary school years and, sometimes, even in high school, long after the late-talking child has begun speaking just fine. This is because even after the talking has caught up for that child, it will usually remain as a relative weakness, especially when compared to analytical thinking abilities. Teachers *know* that the late-talking child can think, but can be at a loss as to why they have trouble learning some subjects.

When my late talking son was a sophomore in high school, his history teacher called me and said, "Your son is not trying in my class; he's a slacker." Because he is one of those children who usually tries hard, I knew that the teacher's impression must have another explanation. I asked the teacher why he thought my son wasn't giving his best effort. The teacher's answer is instructive: "I know he can learn the material because he gets an A on the tests, but he gets low scores on the weekly quizzes. He needs to try harder all the time." I then asked the teacher what material was on the quizzes and on the monthly tests and learned that the quizzes were on the in-class lectures but the exams were based on the reading assignments. So I offered the teacher another reason for this inconsistent performance: "This student talked late, and he still has some trouble learning and remembering during lectures, especially if the topics in the lectures are not in the readings. He remembers much better when he reads something."

The teacher was great, and after he understood the differences in my son's ability to learn by listening and in visual learning (reading), he went the extra mile to ensure my late-talking son now had extra time to learn the in-class lecture material and provided readings for the quizzes. But along with my own background as a late-talking child, and my experience helping my own late-talking child in school, there are the thousands of families we have seen over the years indicating this pattern happens all the time.

Good teachers pick up on the fact that a late-talking child is smart but that they aren't getting some information that is usually mastered by other children who are similarly intelligent. But, because teachers unconsciously use complex language that often overextends the auditory comprehension (learning by listening) abilities of a late-talking child; they are unaware of why there are learning gaps in late-talking children. As with my late-talking son's history teacher, this can sometimes generate negative views of the late-talking child as a slacker, or in many cases, "ADHD," "behavior problem," "learning disabled," or some other incorrect reason for the uneven performance.

To be sure, some late-talking children do have ADHD, behavior problems or learning disabilities, but many more simply are showing a common learning pattern that gets misidentified in school. Parents must be ready to help the teacher understand that nearly all late-talking children will show this kind of weakness in "learning by listening" so that the teacher does not attribute this performance to poor motivation, inattention, or some other negative trait in their child.

But be forewarned, this is easier said than done. After all, the teacher is used to relying on a lecture format that works pretty well with the majority of their other pupils. And most teachers I have worked with are unaware of just how much verbal instruction or how much complicated language is used in their lectures.

When my late-talking son entered kindergarten, I met with his teacher the week before classes started. I told her about late-talking children and how hard it can be for them to learn by a "sit still and listen" teaching approach. At our six-week parent-teacher meeting, she told me "You may not know this, but I think your son has real problems understanding what I say." To her credit, she figured this out by observing him while she was teaching. On the other hand, it made me realize that teachers may not fully grasp what late talking can mean in their everyday lessons, even when they have been told beforehand. I also suspect that teachers, especially those at the kindergarten level, are used to parents telling them many things about their child's learning skills, so that my descriptions may not have been particularly salient to her.

Regardless, a late-talking child's learning patterns are often quite different from other children in the class, so teaching approaches that work well with most children will often be ineffective. When this happens, even well-meaning teachers will then look to *child* characteristics, and not teaching style, as the reason for failure. It *must* be something wrong with late-talking child; after all, "sit still and listen" does work for many children. In schools, parents will have to both keep an eye on the teaching style in the class while also helping the teacher to understand the different learning style of their late-talking child.

Here are a number of strategies we often recommend for navigating schools.

1. Find a school with the *least* emphasis on teaching by listening. Learning by doing and discovery should be the primary approach. Many families report that "alternative schools" such as Montessori, Waldorf, and math/science schools (including charter schools) are a good match for their late-talking child. Don't be put off by the "alternative" label; it is very likely your late-talking child will do far better in schools that do not teach using a "sit still and listen" approach.

2. It is also better if the school does not expect all children to be learning "at grade level" in all subjects. Students should be permitted to work ahead in math and science while being allowed to learn more slowly in subjects more closely aligned with verbal skills (such as reading). Schools that treat students as if they

are on an automotive assembly line are *not* a good match for a late-talking child. The teacher may be trying to figuratively "put tires" on a car that does not yet have wheels!

3. The teacher herself is a very important consideration. A late-talking child can learn in different kinds of schools *if* the teacher is willing to adjust their style to the student's needs and aptitudes. Good teachers do this naturally with all their students. Look for a teacher who talks positively about the students. Avoid teachers who are rigid or find reasons why your child won't do well in their class. Recall the story of the late-talking "math whiz" who was labeled a behavior problem in grade school. His teacher was more concerned about whether he was doing the same thing as the other children in class than she was with teaching what he was ready to learn. Subsequent teachers were very excited about helping develop his mathematical ability rather than trying to hold him back.

4. Always bear in mind that the goal of teaching is "content." Seek schools that are focused on what your child learns, and are dedicated to helping them learn. Avoid classrooms and schools that mistakenly believe that all children must comply with "sit still and listen" and capricious rules in order to learn. This is not a new problem. Winston Churchill, who may well have talked late himself, wrote about his early school experiences in *My Early Life.* "My teachers saw me at once backwards and precocious, reading books beyond my years and yet at the bottom of the Form [class ranking]. They were offended. They had large resources of compulsion at their disposal, but I was stubborn. Where [whenever] my reason, imagination or interest were not engaged, I would not or I could not learn."[5] Prime Minister Churchill was writing about his school experiences of more than 125 years ago, but his words are still highly relevant. Seek

engaging, encouraging, and flexible classrooms that engage your late-talking child's "reason, imagination and intellect." Avoid those with "large resources of compulsion."

5. Help your late-talking child to develop their own techniques for learning. Try to get the lessons, or at least information on the general topic being taught, *ahead* of time. Introduce the knowledge *before* it is taught in class. Your late-talking child will learn much better if they have some advance knowledge of what is coming. I thoroughly enjoyed my time spent with my own late-talking son learning upcoming material. It was especially helpful to get a "key vocabulary" list from the teacher ahead of time. This is usually available in teacher's editions of the textbooks. Some families tell me that they purchase teacher's editions to tutor upcoming lessons. Others families do what we did successfully with my late-talking child; purchase audio editions of the textbooks so late-talking students can listen at the same time they are reading. The goal here is to empower the late-talking child to get the knowledge in the manner that best suits them and help them figure out how to do this on their own.

6. Finally, be sure to take the long view. There is no reason to panic if you start to receive all kinds of "bad reports" from preschool and early grade school teachers when a late-talking child will not sit in circle time or is "not ready" for kindergarten. I can practically guarantee that such notes home will be forthcoming for your late-talking child, so be prepared. Instead, think about what you want your child to know when they are an adult and work towards that goal at your child's own pace. Take reading as an example. Some late-talking children read early, some read on time, and many, like my late-talking son, take much longer. He didn't know his letter sounds until second grade, quite late relative to "grade standards" and the cause for much consternation

in first grade, and, of course, the obligatory notes home and teacher meetings about the dire consequences of this delay. But he simply wasn't ready to learn his letters for another year.

While enrolling my late-talking son in an extra reading tutoring course at his school, I didn't panic because the *real* goal for learning letters is to eventually read fluently and understand what is being read. I knew that drilling him on letter sounds to meet an arbitrary grade standard was a waste of time and could actually end up with him hating to read. I was confident that he would know his letters at some point before he reached adulthood. In truth, the teachers were partially right because it did take years longer for him to read. To their further horror, when he finally did start reading, my late-talking son showed a preference for comic books and adventure stories rather than schoolbooks on the "summer reading list." He would spend hours writing and drawing his own comic books; something some of teachers told me was a waste of time.

But patience and taking the long view paid off. My late-talking son was a political science major in college and by then read difficult books avidly. I fondly recall driving him back from college for summer break a few years ago when we had a lively discussion about the philosophical premises in several books on political thought.[6] As we talked about what he had read, I could only wonder what his first grade teacher would have thought and whether following her advice to drill the letter sounds— and put him on ADHD medication—when he clearly was simply not ready to learn would have derailed his subsequent love of reading.

The key is remembering that that talking late is often a harbinger of your child's learning style: other things may come late too. So don't panic!

10 Putting It All Together

Let's go back to square one and summarize the territory we have covered. We began with a child who was late in talking; usually for some apparently inexplicable reason in the case of children for whom there was no physical or mental abnormality. Often, at that point, there are anxious parents who wondered if there was something they had done, or hadn't done, that caused the problem.

There is no evidence that this is the case and considerable evidence that biology is involved, though scientists are still trying to sort out the specific ways that genes and the organization of the brain operate as factors in the case of when the late talking is a normal *stage* in development with no long-lasting problems or a *symptom* of more general impairments such as intellectual disabilities or autism.

What is most important to a parent at this point—and to the future of the child—is determining whether the late talking is simply a *stage* that the child is passing through or a *symptom* of deeper and longer-lasting problems. Trying to find a reliable answer to that question is a major challenge but one that can be met, if the parents are willing to invest the time and effort to get multiple—and independent—diagnoses from highly qualified professionals. Your pediatrician or family doctor is a good place to start. But, wherever you start, you cannot simply turn your child over to "experts" and rely blindly on what they say—least of all when it is someone who acts imperious and dismisses out of hand a parent's observations and questions. Unfortunately, misdiagnoses and mistreatment are all too common.

What is also much too common are relatives, neighbors, and friends chiming in with their conclusions, advice, and pronouncements. Parents need to tell them, perhaps gently but certainly firmly, that their well-intentioned advice is usually not helpful at all, but is simply creating more stress.

A number of things are known about late-talking children, even if we cannot yet explain all these things. Foremost, we know that in at least 60 percent of the cases, the late talking is not a symptom of autism, apraxia, developmental disabilities, or other dire conditions. Parents should never assume late-talking children will catch up on their own, but the clinician evaluating their child should certainly know that late talking is not automatically a symptom of autism or another long-lasting problem. We know too that the great majority of late-talking children are boys. We know also that most late-talking children tend to be a year or so behind other children when it comes to toilet training and that attempting to rush anything, including toilet training, can be very difficult. In addition, scientific studies of brain images indicate that late-talking children with no apparent medical abnormality—seem to have their speech controlled from different regions of the brain than most other people.

It has been my observation, over the years, that late-talking children tend to be strong-willed, and scientific data indicate that most have stronger visual reasoning than verbal abilities and therefore learn better by doing than by listening. Their strong will and learning style often clash with the teaching styles of most schools, especially in preschool and kindergarten. The problems created by this mismatch continue long after these children have learned to speak. Parents need to stay engaged with the child's school, long after speech and language delays are a thing of the past.

Most late-talking children have neither autism nor the high IQ form of late talking called Einstein syndrome. Yet the parents of children who fall into either of these categories need to understand what these conditions entail. Moreover, all parents of late-talking children need to understand the cryptic phrases sometimes used by clinicians and educators alike—phrases that often conceal or mislead, rather than inform. "Severe developmental delay," for example, often means that the child has intellectual disabilities (formerly called mental retardation), and "pervasive developmental disorder" or "social deficits" are often roundabout ways of saying autism. Parents need to ask directly, in plain English: "Are you saying that my child has intellectual disabilities?" or "Are you saying that my child has autism?" The stakes are too high to let a fog of words cloud the situation. You also need to let people know that you are not there to be talked down to. When you encounter clinicians who dismiss what you have seen your child do, with your own eyes, it is time to go find somebody else who will listen. Parents may not always agree with a clinician's view of their late-talking child, but they and their child should always be treated with respect.

Fortunately, there are legal protections for parents' rights in the public schools. But those protections are only as good as the parents' knowledge of those protections and their willingness to assert those rights. Many parents report positive experiences with the schools—but not always. And sometimes, the parents get the booklet advising them of their rights only after they arrive at the individualized educational program (IEP) meeting where the school authorities announce the decisions they have already made as to where a child is going to be placed, presenting parents with a *fait accompli*.

Also, there are organizations that will help parents assert their rights, including national, state, and local disability rights groups. School officials have been known to change their tune completely when they find themselves confronted by parents who will not be intimidated and who refuse to go along with preordained "self-contained" classrooms and cookie-cutter goals and treatments—and, most importantly, who refuse to sign away both their parental rights and their child's future.

While parents should be prepared to deal with people whose policies or actions can be detrimental to their child, they should also be aware that there are many individual educators and whole schools—and sometimes whole school systems—that are more understanding and more flexible. There are terrific schools, teachers, and clinicians: parents face the task of seeking them out.

Parents of children with the Einstein syndrome face special problems. Schools for gifted children are especially hard to find in the public school systems of most cities, New York's Stuyvesant High School and Brooklyn Tech being rare exceptions. On the other hand, parents of children with the Einstein syndrome need to be aware that some universities have summer programs for unusually bright children—Purdue, Johns Hopkins, and Duke Universities come to mind, as does the Duke University summer youth programs for "academically motivated youth." I have taught in the program at Purdue and my Vanderbilt colleagues Camilla Benbow and David Lubinski, both noted authorities on the education of gifted children, have taught there and at Iowa

State University, with Professor Benbow also having taught at Johns Hopkins.

In addition, there are colleges and universities that will admit a very bright student before he or she completes high school, providing yet another escape for students who might otherwise be stifled in their public high school. But these are all exceptional things—though things well worth seeking out by parents whose children's very brightness can be a handicap in a rigid educational setting.

Unfortunately, parents of late-talking children in general may encounter people, whether educators or clinicians, who have gotten used to dealing with parents who are frightened for their children's future, vulnerable, and sometimes desperate, and so will do whatever they're told will solve their children's baffling problem. Some even exploit this situation to extract substantial sums of money for treatments that are dubious or even demonstrably bogus. Other well-meaning professionals make earnest attempts to help the children but may lack the level of knowledge required to cope with what can be a complex problem and rely instead on the prevailing dogmas, fashions, or groupthink of their peers.

Many clinicians who directly evaluate and treat children may be unfamiliar with current research on the many problems of late-talking children and may provide diagnoses or treatments that are unproven or even discredited. There may be a large amount of scientific literature disproving some of the things these ground-level clinicians believe and practice, but that literature can remain largely unread by most practitioners, simply because it may be inaccessible to people without the requisite training in science or their caseload may be so large there is no time to keep up with the latest discoveries. Therefore much of the careful research of dedicated scholars remains like the proverbial tree that falls in an empty forest, as far as actual clinical practice is concerned.

All too many clinicians seem to assume that there *must* be something wrong when a child talks late and end up conducting an evaluation that *confirms* this assumption. As discussed earlier, parents need to know up front whether the evaluation is designed to provide *differential* diagnosis among the different conditions for which late talking is a symptom, or is simply designed to make a child eligible for services or an early intervention or special education program. Parents should *always* ask whether clinician thinks that late talking could ever be a passing stage. And, after a diagnosis has been given, parents should *always* ask whether any other conditions have been ruled out. In particular, when an autism diagnosis is given, ask whether the clinician tested for social communication disorder and directly ask about the severity rating for the autism. When an intellectual disability diagnosis is given, ask whether the test given required verbal questions and answers and, if so, request that a nonverbal intelligence test be given.

It is simply not possible for any professional organization to have both the clout and the will to impose standards of treatment that would drive out charlatans and incompetents. After all, even rigorous medical school training and the American Medical Association have not be able to stop the Defeat Autism Now physicians from practicing even though their methods for treating autism have been questionable at best.[1] It is easy to see how this can happen.

For example, I recommend that all late-talking children be evaluated by a speech pathologist because these specialists have graduate level training on how to diagnose and treat speech and language disorders in children. But, I have been to conventions of the American Speech-Language-Hearing Association where there were exhibits promoting treatments based on theories that had already been questioned, again and again, in scientific studies published in the journals of this very association.

For example, parents tell me about speech clinics that seem to diagnose *all* late-talking children as having apraxia even though the scientific studies on this condition show that it is quite rare.[2] Worse, the apraxia diagnosis all too often is then used as a justification for oral-motor exercises such as blowing whistles even though such exercises have been criticized as being unnecessary in the scientific literature on treating speech disorders in children.[3] But, clinicians have told me that they learned these techniques in graduate school or in workshops that provide professional continuing education credits and purchased the therapy materials at exhibitor booths at the national speech convention. How would they know that these techniques are discredited? These clinicians also tell me they have a high success rate in their practices. Of course, as a clinical scientist, I would expect a high "success" rate unless the tongue and blowing exercises are harmful (which they do not seem to be) because if all late-talking children are misdiagnosed as having apraxia, *at least* 60 percent will get better in a year or two on their own! The disconnect between clinical scientists and practitioners can be striking.

Of course, this problem is by no means limited to speech specialists. Now that Andrew Wakefield's study linking autism to vaccines has been withdrawn from *The Lancet*[4] and the prestigious *British Medical Journal* has suggested the study was fraudulent,[5] shouldn't treatments based on this research be banned? Dr. Wakefield's medical license was revoked in England, but it is anyone's guess as to how many clinics and clinicians are still providing treatments based on his discredited research on autism and vaccines. The American Medical Association should be providing much clearer information to parents regarding which treatments are, and more importantly, are not, supported by credible scientific evidence.

Parents need to have their eyes open to the realities of the labyrinth they enter when they seek help for a child who is late in talking, whether they are seeking help from private clinical practitioners or from the public educational system. This is not to say that the situation is all bleak or hopeless, by any means. There are many earnest and dedicated professionals at all levels. And the odds are favorable that families will encounter one of these. But, very few of the scholars doing the research are likely to directly treat late-talking children, face to face, on a regular basis, as distinguished from studying samples of such children as part of their research.

Among the ground-level practitioners who do directly treat children on a regular basis, a good speech pathologist can be very helpful—as can special educators, autism specialists, and other teachers and clinicians. Unfortunately, there are all too many who are not helpful, and sadly, some who can be harmful. How many fall into which category is a matter of speculation. Sadly, a subjective rating places the odds at only 50–50 that an accurate diagnosis and proper treatment program at the ground level. This is why parents have to learn to try to pick their way through a minefield and be cautious when seeking answers about whether the late talking is a symptom or a stage.

People who make policies, whether in government agencies or in professional organizations like the American Speech-Language-Hearing Association, the American Academy of Pediatrics, and the American Medical Association, need to adopt policies and practices that improve the odds for parents and for the children whose futures are at stake.

What Parents Should Know

Perhaps the most tragic "side effect" of late talking—regardless of whether a symptom or a stage—is that worry about what it can mean all too often robs parents, especially mothers, of precious memories of their child's toddler and preschool years. Even when the late talking is a symptom, it is important to love and nurture your child, celebrating and savoring the victories. *No matter what, don't ever forget to enjoy your precious child!* These years pass all too quickly and the time is irreplaceable.

The situation is especially regrettable when the late talking is actually a stage rather than a symptom. I recall one mother recounting how she stayed awake night after night searching the Internet for answers while worrying about her late-talking son. She told me that his toddler years were just a blur; anxiety crowded out memories of first steps, first and second birthdays, and so many other milestones that parents usually cherish. Worse, she reported reading on credible websites that angelic faces, with cute round cheeks like cherubs, is some kind of marker for childhood apraxia of speech. Of course, this is nonsense, but her own little boy was very cute, with a sweet "cherub" face. But now, what should have been a source of laughter and joy became a "symptom" of apraxia for her. I have monitored this little boy's speech development since he was a toddler—he is now in second grade—and it is absolutely inarguable that he does *not and never did* have apraxia. I note here that he never received "apraxia treatment," so it is simply not possible that this was somehow "cured" along the way by early intervention. But until he started talking at around the age of three, even seeing photos of his cute, angelic "cherub" face brought his mother to tears! And these weren't the tears of joy and happiness they should have been.

Remember the key points discussed throughout this book:

1. Always get a medical evaluation and a developmental evaluation for your late-talking child. Never assume your child is necessarily one of the 60 percent or more—who catch up in a year or two. But do not leave your common sense at the door when you get an evaluation. Ask questions—and get answers. Don't be afraid to ask, "Do you think my child will ever catch up?" Keep in mind that it is far better for a clinician to respond truthfully: "I don't know," than to confidently provide inaccurate answers. If the clinician acts as if questions are an affront to his or her authority, proclamations and pronouncements, seek another clinician. Finally, a skilled clinician will not only tell you about what is wrong and what a child can't do, but should also discuss your late-talking child's strengths too.

2. There are many well-trained and highly skilled clinicians available to help when the late talking is a symptom rather than a stage. Seek these out and follow their advice. There are schools, treatment centers, and programs that can help too. Find the clinicians and teachers that have a positive attitude towards you and your late-talking child. Unfortunately, there are also clinicians who are less skilled or misinformed and, of course, there are outright charlatans. Parents need to arm themselves with the information and common sense to tell the difference.

3. Never blindly accept a diagnosis. Ask the clinician how the diagnosis was generated and whether the evaluation was conducted simply to confirm eligibility for autism or to differentiate between the different conditions for which late talking is a symptom. I always ask parents if what I am seeing in their late-talking child matches what they know about their child. If parents disagree with what I say, as sometimes happens, this is not an invitation to claim they are in denial. Rather, a skilled

clinician will explain how they arrived at the diagnosis and listen to what the parents have to say.

4. If given an autism diagnosis, ask how severe it is and whether it could be language disorder, speech disorder or social communication disorder instead. If "PDD-NOS" or "Asperger syndrome" is diagnosed in any late-talking child, it means that the clinician is not using the current diagnostic protocol (the American Psychiatric Association's 2013 *DSM5*). Finally, do not accept questionable diagnoses such as "processing disorder" or "sensory integration deficit" that are not widely accepted or have questionable validity.[6] All too often, these questionable diagnoses are simply a way of justifying a controversial or unproven treatment.

5. Speaking of treatment, parents should always be offered an opportunity to be a central part of treatment rather than be treated as part of the problem. Some parents are not able to work with their late-talking child for various reasons, and that is fine. But the opportunity should be offered nonetheless. It should *not* be mandatory to enroll a late-talking child in day care or preschool. If parents are up to it and either or both can stay with their child at home, this is often a good option, and the clinician should be willing to help them learn what to do.[7]

6. Treatment should focus directly on learning to talk, and, if needed, to teach a late-talking child to understand what is said. Avoid therapies that promise to "unlock" or "retrain" the brain using tones, metronomes or brain training computer games. Be especially wary of treatments that can be touted for a whole bunch of different problems. An advertisement that promotes a therapy that purportedly "works with ADHD, stuttering, autism, learning disabilities, as well as head injuries" is a waste of time and money.

7. There are no special diets—such as those that are "gluten free;" vitamins—for example, fish oil (EFA) or vitamin B12; computer software; medication (prescription or over the counter); chelation; oral motor exercises; brushing or wearing a weighted or compression vest; or any other treatment such as these that will help a child learn to talk. I can practically guarantee that these and other fringe "cures" will be touted by well-meaning but misinformed clinicians—as well as outright charlatans—and vetted by other parents of late-talking children who have seen their own children "recover" after receiving one or more of these treatments. If it sounds too good to be true, it almost certainly is. There are no magic bullets or quick fixes if the late talking turns out to be a symptom.

8. You are not alone! Although your late-talking child may be the only one in the neighborhood, in fact, there are many other families whose child shares traits with yours. These families can be a great source of support and information. There is a parent moderated bulletin board at latetalkkids@yahoogroups.com. In addition, the website for the Foundation for Families of Late-Talking Children (latetalkers.org) includes useful information. You should also seek out other families in your area since they may know of programs, doctors, and clinicians that are helpful in seeking answers for your late-talking child.

9. No matter who sees your child, be it a physician, a specialist such as a speech pathologist, psychologist, or occupational therapist, or special educator or classroom teacher, everyone should treat you—and your child—with respect, including a respect for basic human rights. Never let anyone unjustly impose their will on you, or your late-talking child in the name of a "cure." Do not allow anyone to strap your child in a chair or restrain them in name of forcing them to talk or "comply" with clinician or

teacher directives. A parent's primary responsibility is to look out for their child's safety, and late-talking children are especially vulnerable.

One final note to parents: trust your common sense! If you hear your child screaming while they are in therapy or in school, find out what's going on immediately. And don't be afraid to take them out if you don't agree with what is happening. Do not let anyone talk you into something you are uneasy or unsure about. Never forget that you know your late-talking child better than anyone else.

Notes

Chapter 1

1. Sue Woolfenden, Vanessa Sarkozy, Greta Ridley, and Katrina Williams, "A Systematic Review of the Diagnostic Stability of Autism Spectrum Disorder, *Research in Autism Spectrum Disorders* 6, no. 1 (2012): 345–354.

2. Zachary Warren, Melissa L. McPheeters, Nila Sathe, Jennifer H. Foss-Feig, Allison Glasser, and Jeremy Veenstra-VanderWeele, "A Systematic Review of Early Intensive Intervention for Autism Spectrum Disorders," *Pediatrics* 127, no. 5 (2011): e1303–e1311 (quote on p. 1303).

3. Josephine Barbaro and Cheryl Dissanayake, "Autism Spectrum Disorders in Infancy and Toddlerhood: A Review of the Evidence on Early Signs, Early Identification Tools, and Early Diagnosis," *Journal of Developmental & Behavioral Pediatrics* 30, no. 5 (2009): 447–459.

4. Leslie Rescorla and Thomas M. Achenbach, "Use of the Language Development Survey (LDS) in a National Probability Sample of Children 18 to 35 Months Old," *Journal of Speech, Language and Hearing Research* 45, no. 4 (2002): 733–743.

5. Leslie Rescorla and Philip Dale, *Late Talkers* (Baltimore: Brookes Publishing, 2013).

6. Steven Pinker, *The Language Instinct* (New York: William Morrow and Company, 1994), 289. Performing the function of speech is not simply

a matter of controlling the tongue and vocal chords, but involves the more complex task of *formulating* language—a task performed with sign language by those unable to hear or speak, as well as by others using vocal speech. The fact that this task is performed almost automatically, through habit, by most adults does not make it an easy thing to learn to do for the first time as a small child (ibid., 302).

7. Karsten Johanson, *A History of Ancient Philosophy* (London: Routledge, 1998), 324.

8. See, for example, L. Portney and M. Watkins, *Foundations of Clinical Research: Applications to Practice*, 3rd ed. (Upper Saddle River, NJ: Pearson, 2008).

Chapter 2

1. Laurence B. Leonard, "Is Expressive Language Disorder an Accurate Diagnostic Category?," *American Journal of Speech-Language Psychology* 18 (May 2009): 115–123 (especially p. 120).

2. Philip Dale and Marianna Hayiou-Thomas. "Outcomes for Late Talkers," in Leslie Rescorla and Philip Dale, eds., *Late Talkers* (Baltimore, MD: Paul H. Brookes Publishing, 2013), 241–257 (quote on p. 241).

3. Edith Bavin and Lesley Bretherton, "The Early Language in Victoria Study," in Rescorla and Dale, eds., *Late Talkers*, 3–21.

4. Philip S. Dale, Thomas S. Price, Dorothy V. M. Bishop, and Robert Plomin, "Outcomes of Early Language Delay: I. Predicting Persistent and Transient Language Difficulties at 3 and 4 Years," *Journal of Speech, Language and Hearing Research* 46, no. 3 (2003): 544–560 (quote on p. 544).

5. Janet E. Fischel, Grover J. Whitehurst, Marie B. Caulfield, and Barbara DeBaryshe. "Language Growth in Children with Expressive Language Delay," *Pediatrics* 83, no. 2 (1989): 218–227.

6. Leslie Rescorla, "Age 17 Language and Reading Outcomes in Late-Talking Toddlers: Support for a Dimensional Perspective on Language Delay," *Journal of Speech, Language and Hearing Research* 52, no. 1 (2009): 16–30 (quote on p. 23).

7. Rescorla, "Age 17 Language and Reading Outcomes," 26

8. Rhea Paul and Susan Ellis-Weismer, "Late Talking in Context: The Clinical Implications of Delayed Language Development," in Rescorla and Dale, eds., *Late Talkers*, 203–217.

9. Leonard, "Is Expressive Language Disorder an Accurate Diagnostic Category?"

10. Judy Flax, Teresa Realpe-Bonilla, Cynthia Roesler, Naseem Choudhury, and April Benasich, "Using Early Standard Language Measures to Predict Later Language and Early Reading Outcomes in Children at Risk for Language-Learning Impairments," *Journal of Learning Disabilities* 42 (2009): 61–75 (quote on p. 61 and see also p. 72).

11. Paul and Ellis-Weismer, "Late Talking in Context."

12. Dorothy V. M. Bishop, "What Causes Specific Language Impairment in Children?," *Current Directions in Psychological Science* 15, no. 5 (October 2006): 217–221 (quote on 217).

13. Ibid., 218.

14. Ibid., 217.

15. J. Bruce Tomblin, Nancy L. Records, Paula Buckwalter, Xuyang Zhang, Elaine Smith, and Marlea O'Brien, "Prevalence of Specific Language Impairment in Kindergarten Children," *Journal of Speech-Language-Hearing Research* 40 (December 1997): 1245–1260.

16. Sharynne McLeod and Linda J. Harrison, "Epidemiology of Speech and Language Impairment in a Nationally Representative Sample of 4- to 5-Year-Old Children," *Journal of Speech, Language, and Hearing Research* 52, no. 5 (October 2009): 1213–1229; D. Keating, G. Turrell, and A. Ozanne, "Childhood Speech Disorders: Reported Prevalence, Comorbidity and Socioeconomic Profile," *Journal of Paediatrics and Child Health* 37, no. 5 (October 2001): 431–436; Sarah McCue Horwitz, Julia R. Irwin, Margaret J. Briggs-Gowan, Joan M. Bosson Heenan, Jennifer Mendoza, and Alice S. Carter, "Language Delay in a Community Cohort of Young Children," *Journal of the American Academy of Child & Adolescent Psychiatry* 42, no. 8 (August 2003): 932–940.

17. Thomas Sowell, *The Einstein Syndrome* (New York: Basic Books, 2001), 14–15.

18. Martin Fujiki, Bonnie Briton, Craig Hart, and April Fitzgerald, "Peer Acceptance and Friendships in Children with Specific Language Impairment, *Topics in Language Disorders* 19 (1999): 34–48.

19. I have not only seen this in late-talking children who come to my clinic, I remember that I was this way myself as a young late talker. When the children in my class were asked to spell the names of numbers up to 10, I simply refused to do it, and a note was sent home to my mother, who knew that I knew how to spell those numbers. She came to school and told me to spell the numbers up to 10 or she would spank me! I then spelled the numbers—and threw in the spelling of other numbers, up to a million. Needless to say, my teacher was shocked to learn I knew how to do this. Like many late-talking children, I did not like to "perform on demand" in school.

20. Rescorla, "Age 17 Language and Reading Outcomes."

21. Andrew J. O. Whitehouse and Dorothy V. M. Bishop, "Cerebral Dominance for Language Function in Adults with Specific Language Impairment or Autism," *Brain* (2008): 3193–3200 (quote on p. 254); also see Byron Bernal and Nolan R. Altman, "Speech Delay in Children: A Functional MR Imaging Study," *Radiology* (December 2003): 651–658.

22. Whitehouse and Bishop, "Cerebral Dominance for Language Function in Adults with Specific Language Impairment or Autism."

23. Ibid.

24. Diane F. Halpern, *Sex Differences in Cognitive Abilities* (Hillsdale, NJ: Erlbaum, 1986), 82.

25. Deborah Blum, *Sex on the Brain: The Biological Differences between Men and Women* (New York: Penguin Books, 1997), 61.

26. Ibid., 53.

27. Diane F. Halpern, *Sex Differences in Cognitive Abilities*, 48.

28. Gina Kolata, "Men and Women Use Brain Differently, Study Discovers," *New York Times*, February 16, 1995, A1; Bennet A. Shaywitze et al., "Sex Differences in the Functional Organization of the Brain for Language," *Nature* 373, no. 16 (February 1995), 607–609; Deborah Blum, *Sex on the Brain*, 59, 61.

29. J. S. Hyde and N. McKinley (1997). "Gender Differences in Cognition: Results from Meta-analyses," in *Gender Differences in Human Cognition,* ed. J. S. Hyde and J. Richardson (New York: Oxford University Press), 30–51; C. P. Benbow and J. C. Stanley, "Sex Differences in Mathematical Reasoning Ability: Fact or Artifact?," *Science* 210 (1980): 1262–1264.

30. S. Camarata and R. Woodcock, "Sex Differences in Processing Speed: Developmental Effects in Males and Females," *Intelligence* 84 (2006): 231–252.

31. http://www.nsf.gov/statistics/seind14/index.cfm/chapter-3/c3h .htm#s1.

32. Sowell, *The Einstein Syndrome*, 14–15.

33. Ibid., 5–7.

34. http://www.bls.gov/ooh/entertainment-and-sports/musicians-and -singers.htm

35. Thomas Sowell, *Late-Talking Children* (New York: Basic Books, 1997), 83.

36. Karin Stromswold, "The Genetics of Speech and Language Impairments," *New England Journal of Medicine* 359 (2008): 2381–2383.

37. Ibid., 2381.

38. Ibid., 2381–2383.

39. *Dorland's Medical Dictionary*, 31st ed. (Philadelphia: Elsevier Press, 2010).

40. Karen Forrest, "Diagnostic Criteria of Developmental Apraxia of Speech Used by Clinical Speech-Language Pathologists," *American Journal of Speech-Language Pathology* 12, no. 3 (2003). Quote on p. 376.

41. G. Lof, "The Nonspeech Oral Motor Exercise Phenomenon in Speech Pathology Practice," in C. Bowen, ed., *Children's Speech Sound Disorders*, 81–184 (Oxford: Wiley-Blackwell, 2009).

42. N. Silberberg and M. Silberberg, "Case Histories in Hyperlexia," *Journal of School Psychology* 7, no. 1 (1968): 3.

43. Dennis Whitehouse and James C. Harris, "Hyperlexia in Infantile Autism," *Journal of Autism and Developmental Disorders* 14, no. 3 (September 1984): 281–289 (quote on 281).

Chapter 3

1. Daniela Caruso, "Autism in the US: Social Movement and Legal Change, *American Journal of the Law & Medicine* 36 (2010): 483.

2. Paul T. Shattuck, "The Contribution of Diagnostic Substitution to the Growing Administrative Prevalence of Autism in US Special Education," *Pediatrics* 117, no. 4 (2006): 1028–1037.

3. Dorothy V. M. Bishop, Andrew J. O. Whitehouse, Helen J. Watt, and Elizabeth A. Line, "Autism and Diagnostic Substitution: Evidence from a Study of Adults with a History of Developmental Language Disorder," *Developmental Medicine & Child Neurology* 50, no. 5 (2008): 341–345.

4. L. Kanner, "Autistic Disturbances of Affective Conduct," *Nervous Child* 2 (1943): 217–250; my italics.

5. Ibid., 246; original italics.

6. F. Volkmar, D. Cohen, and R. Paul, "An Evaluation of DSM-III Criteria for Infantile Autism," *Journal of the American Academy of Child Psychiatry* 25 (1986): 190–197 (quote on p. 190).

7. Saasha Sutera, Juhi Pandey, Emma L. Esser, Michael A. Rosenthal, Leandra B. Wilson, Marianne Barton, James Green, et al, "Predictors of Optimal Outcome in Toddlers Diagnosed With Autism Spectrum Disorders," Journal of Autism and Developmental Disorders 37, no. 1 (2007): 98–107.

8. Catherine Lord, Susan Risi, Pamela S. DiLavore, Cory Shulman, Audrey Thurm, and Andrew Pickles, "Autism from 2 to 9 Years of Age," *Archives of General Psychiatry* 63, no. 6 (2006): 694–701.

9. Eva Billstedt, Carina Gillberg, and Christopher Gillberg, "Autism after Adolescence: Population-Based 13-to 22-Year Follow-up Study of 120 Individuals with Autism Diagnosed in Childhood," Journal of Autism and Developmental Disorders 35, no. 3 (2005): 351–360.

10. Maia Szalavitz, "Aging Out of Autism," Time, February 4, 2013 (quote appears on p. 16).

11. Deborah Fein, Marianne Barton, Inge-Marie Eigsti, Elizabeth Kelley, Letitia Naigles, Robert T. Schultz, and Michael Stevens, et al, "Optimal Outcome in Individuals with a History of Autism." Journal of Child Psychology and Psychiatry 54, no. 2 (2013): 195–205.

12. E. Rondeau, L. Klein, A. Masse, N. Bodeau, D. Cohen, and J. Guile, "Is Pervasive Developmental Disorder Not Otherwise Specified Less Stable Than Autistic Disorder? A Meta-Analysis," *Journal of Autism Developmental Disorders* 41, no. 9 (September 2010), doi:10.1007/s10803-010-1155-z.

13. Ibid.

14. L. Kanner, "Infantile Autism and the Schizophrenias," *Behavioral Science* 10 (1965): 412–420 (quote on p. 413).

15. Ibid.

16. American Psychiatric Association, "Social (Pragmatic) Communication Disorder" (2013), http://www.dsm5.org/Documents/Social%20Communication%20Disorder%20Fact%20Sheet.pdf.

17. Catherine Lord, Eva Petkova, Vanessa Hus, Weijin Gan, Feihan Lu, Donna M. Martin, Opal Ousley, et al, "A Multisite Study of the Clinical Diagnosis of Different Autism Spectrum Disorders," *Archives of General Psychiatry*: 69, no 3 (2011): 306–313 (quote on p. 312).

18. Mona Al-Qabandi, Jan Willem Gorter, and Peter Rosenbaum, "Early Autism Detection: Are We Ready for Routine Screening? *Pediatrics* 128, no. 1 (2011): e211–e217 (quote on p. 211).

19. Bright Futures/American Academy of Pediatrics, "Recommendations for Preventive Pediatric Health Care," 2014, http://www.aap.org/en-us/professional-resources/practice-support/Periodicity/PeriodicitySchedule _Final.pdf.

20. Wendy L. Stone, Evon B. Lee, Linda Ashford, Jane Brissie, Susan L. Hepburn, Elaine E. Coonrod, and Bahr H. Weis, "Can Autism Be Diagnosed Accurately in Children under 3 Years?" *Journal of Child Psychology and Psychiatry* 40, no. 2 (1999): 219–226.

21. Ellen Winner, *Gifted Children: Myths and Realities* (New York: Basic Books, 1996), 27–29.

22. Ibid., 30, 218.

23. Ibid., 29.

24. Thomas Sowell, *The Einstein Syndrome: Bright Children Who Talk Late* (New York: Basic Books), 2001.

25. Lorna Wing et al., "The Prevalence of Early Childhood Autism: Comparison of Administrative and Epidemiological Studies," *Psychological Medicine: A Journal of Research in Psychiatry and the Allied Sciences* 6, no. 1 (February 1976): 89–110.

26. Michael D. Kogan, "Prevalence of Parent-Reported Diagnosis of Autism Spectrum Disorder among Children in the U.S., 2007," *Pediatrics* 124, no. 5 (November 2009): 1395–1403.

27. Paul T. Shattuck, "The Contribution of Diagnostic Substitution to the Growing Administrative Prevalence of Autism."

28. Helen Coo, Helene Ouellette-Kuntz, Jennifer E. V. Lloyd, Liza Kasmara, Jeanette J. A. Holden, and M. E. Suzanne Lewis, "Trends in Autism Prevalence: Diagnostic Substitution Revisited," *Journal of Autism and Developmental Disorders* 38, no. 6 (2008): 1036–1046 (quote on p. 1036).

29. Margot Prior, "Is There an Increase in the Prevalence of Autism Spectrum Disorders?," *Journal of Paediatrics and Child Health* 39, no. 2 (2003): 81–82 (quote on p. 81).

30. J. Saracino, J. Noseworthy, M. Steiman, L. Reisinger, and E. Fombonne, "Diagnostic and Assessment Issues in Autism Surveillance and

Prevalence," *Journal of Developmental and Physical Abilities* 22 (2010): 317–330.

31. Paul Offit, *Autism's False Prophets* (New York: Columbia University Press, 2008).

Chapter 4

1. Patricia Howlin. "Prognosis in Autism: Do Specialist Treatments Affect Long-Term Outcome?," *European Child & Adolescent Psychiatry* 6, no. 2 (1997): 55–72.

2. Catherine Lord, Ann Wagner, Sally Rogers, Peter Szatmari, Michael Aman, Tony Charman, and Geraldine Dawson, et al, "Challenges in Evaluating Psychosocial Interventions for Autistic Spectrum Disorders," *Journal of Autism and Developmental Disorders* 35, no. 6 (2005): 695–708 (quote on p. 696).

3. John Green, Overview: "Detoxification in Chelation Therapy." In *Recovering Autistic Children*, eds. Stephen M. Edelson and Bernard Rimland, 2nd ed. (San Diego, CA: Autism Research Institute, 2006), 433-436 (quote on p. 433).

4. Ibid., 435.

5. Trine Tsouderos, *Chicago Tribune*, October 14, 2010, http://articles .chicagotribune.com/2010-10-14/health/ct-met-fda-autism-chelation -20101014_1_chelators-autism-treatment-metal-poisoning; http://www.fda.gov/Drugs/ResourcesForYou/Consumers/ BuyingUsingMedicineSafely/MedicationHealthFraud/ucm229313.htm.

6. http://www.fda.gov/Drugs/ResourcesForYou/Consumers/ BuyingUsingMedicineSafely/MedicationHealthFraud/ucm229313.htm.

7. Patricia Howlin, "Prognosis in Autism: Do Specialist Treatments Affect Long-Term Outcome?," *European Child & Adolescent Psychiatry* 6, no. 2 (1997): 55–72.

8. Sharon L. Hostler, "Facilitated Communication," *Pediatrics* 97, no. 4 (1996): 584–586 (quote on p. 584). Howard C. Shane, *Facilitated*

Communication: The Clinical and Social Phenomenon (San Diego, CA: Singular Publishing Co.), 1994.

9. Scott M. Myers and Chris Plauché Johnson, "Management of Children with Autism Spectrum Disorders," *Pediatrics* 120, no. 5 (2007): 1162–1182.

10. The Editors of The Lancet, "Retraction—Ileal-Lymphoid-Nodular Hyperplasia, Non-specific Colitis, and Pervasive Developmental Disorder in Children," *The Lancet* 375, no. 9713 (February 2010): 445.

11. Zena Stein, "Autism's False Prophets," *International Journal of Epidemiology* 38, no. 5 (October 2009): 1417.

12. Paul Offit, *Autism's False Prophets* (New York: Columbia University Press, 2008), 42–43.

13. Simon Cottrell and Richard John Roberts, "Measles Outbreak in Europe," *BMJ* 342 (2011).

14. Kate Kelland, "Lancet Retracts Paper Linking Vaccine to Autism," *Washington Post*, February 3, 2010, A2.

15. "The Lancet's Vaccine Retraction," *Wall Street Journal*, February 3, 2010, A16.

16. Nigel Rees, *Why Do We Say…?: Words and Sayings and Where They Come From* (London: Blandford Press), 1987.

17. Even a deadly poison like arsenic, in extremely minute traces in drinking water, has been found to be beneficial.

18. John F. Burns, "British Council Bars Doctor Who Linked Vaccine with Autism," *New York Times*, May 25, 2010, A4.

19. James Bone and David Rose. "MMR Scare Doctor Andrew Wakefield Makes Fortune in US." *The Times* (London), February 14, 2009.

20. Aly Weisman, "16 Things Jenny McCarthy Has Actually Said," Business Insider, July 15, 2013, http://www.businessinsider.com/jenny-mccarthy-the-view-autism-vaccines-controversial-quotes-2013-7#ixzz2gcdflJ6X.

21. Jeffrey Kluger, "Jenny McCarthy on Autism and Vaccines," *Time*, April 1, 2009, http://content.time.com/time/health/article/0,8599,1888718,00.html#ixzz1qFAZnfv9.

22. http://www.nytimes.com/2009/01/13/health/13auti.html?_r=0.

23. Peter Szatmari,, Andrew D. Paterson, Lonnie Zwaigenbaum, Wendy Roberts, Jessica Brian, Xiao-Qing Liu, John B. Vincent, et al. "Mapping Autism Risk Loci Using Genetic Linkage and Chromosomal Rearrangements," *Nature Genetics* 39, no. 3 (2007): 319–328.

24. M. Losh, P. Sullivan, D. Trembath, and J. Piven, "Current Developments in the Genetics of Autism: From Phenome to Genome," *Journal of Neuropathology and Experimental Neurology* 67 (2008): 829–837.

25. R. A. Stevenson, J. K. Siemann, B. C. Schneider, H. E. Eberly, T. G. Woynaroski, S. M. Camarata, and M. T. Wallace, "Multisensory Temporal Integration in Autism Spectrum Disorders," *The Journal of Neuroscience* 34, no. 3 (2014), 691–697.

26. Armin Raznahan, Gregory L. Wallace, Ligia Antezana, Dede Greenstein, Rhoshel Lenroot, Audrey Thurm, Marta Gozzi, et al, "Compared to What? Early Brain Overgrowth in Autism and the Perils of Population Norms," *Biological Psychiatry* 74, no. 8 (2013): 563–575.

27. Shirley Wang, "In the Lab: Scanning Babies for Autism," *Wall Street Journal*, May 25, 2010, D2.

28. Jeffrey P. Baker, "Autism in 1959: Joey the Mechanical Boy." *Pediatrics* 125, no. 6 (2010): 1101–1103.

29. Joachim Hallmayer, Sue Cleveland, Andrea Torres, Jennifer Phillips, Brianne Cohen, Tiffany Torigoe, Janet Miller, et al. "Genetic Heritability and Shared Environmental Factors among Twin Pairs with Autism," *Archives of General Psychiatry* 68, no. 11 (2011): 1095–1102.

30. Ibid.

31. The *Chicago Tribune*, for example, referred to him as someone whose "total residential care" included "acceptance" and "love" (John W. Fountain, "Dr. Bruno Bettelheim, Child Psychology Expert," *Chicago*

Tribune, March 14, 1990, section 2, 14); the *Washington Post*'s obituary praised his "warmth" and "emotional sympathy" (Martin Weil, "Pioneering Psychologist Bruno Bettelheim Dies," *Washington Post*, March 14, 1990, A1); the *New York Times* wrote of his "deep empathy for children" and quoted another psychoanalyst who spoke of Bettelheim's "respect for their dignity" (Daniel Goleman, "Bruno Bettelheim Dies at 86; Psychoanalyst of Vast Impact," *New York Times*, March 14, 1990, A1, D25); *U.S. News & World Report* described him as "permissive with the disturbed children he treated" ("The Special Finesse of 'Doctor Yes,'" *U.S. News & World Report*, March 26, 1990, 16).

32. Charles Pekow, "The Other Dr. Bettelheim: The Revered Psychologist Had a Dark, Violent Side," *Washington Post*, August 20, 1990, C1, C4.

33. Nina Darnton, "Beno Brutalheim?," *Newsweek*, September 10, 1990, 59.

34. Ronald Angres, "Who, Really, Was Bruno Bettelheim?," *Commentary*, October 1990, 27.

35. "Beno Brutalheim?," *Newsweek*, September 10, 1990, 59.

36. Robert L. Koegel and Lynn Kern Koegel, *Pivotal Response Treatments for Autism: Communication, Social, and Academic Development* (Baltimore, MD: Brookes Publishing Company), 2006.

37. Ibid.

38. Koegel and Koegel, *Pivotal Response Treatments for Autism.*

39. Tristram Smith, Svein Eikeseth, Morten Klevstrand, and O. Ivar Lovaas. "Intensive Behavioral Treatment for Preschoolers with Severe Mental Retardation and Pervasive Developmental Disorder." *American Journal on Mental Retardation* 102, no. 3 (1997): 238–249.

40. Heather Gillum, Stephen Camarata, Keith E. Nelson, and Mary N. Camarata, "A Comparison of Naturalistic and Analog Treatment Effects in Children with Expressive Language Disorder and Poor Preintervention Imitation Skills," *Journal of Positive Behavior Interventions* 5, no. 3 (2003): 171–178.

41. Lynn Kern Koegel, "Overcoming Autism: Finding the Answers, Strategies, and Hope that Can Transform a Child's Life" (New York: Penguin Books), 2014; Kogel and Koegel, *Pivotal Response Treatments for Autism.*

42. Sally J. Rogers and Geraldine Dawson, *Early Start Denver Model for Young Children with Autism: Promoting Language, Learning, and Engagement* (New York, NY: Guilford Press), 2010.

43. Kelly Stickles Goods, Eric Ishijima, Ya-Chih Chang, and Connie Kasari, "Preschool Based JASPER Intervention in Minimally Verbal Children with Autism: Pilot RCT," *Journal of Autism and Developmental Disorders* (2012): 1050–1056.

44. O. Ivar Lovaas, "Behavioral Treatment and Normal Educational and Intellectual Functioning in Young Autistic Children," *Journal of Consulting and Clinical Psychology* 55, no. 1 (1987): 3–9.

Chapter 5

1. When famed pianist Arthur Rubinstein was a young child fixated on the family's piano, he screamed and wept when he was asked to leave the drawing room, where the piano was located. When his father bought him a violin to play, the little boy smashed the violin.

2. Thelma E. Weeks, *The Slow Speech Development of a Bright Child* (Lexington, KY: Heath, 1974), 11.

3. Thomas Sowell, *Late-Talking Children* (New York: Basic Books, 1997), 45.

4. Roger Highfield and Paul Carter, *The Private Lives of Albert Einstein* (London: Faber and Faber, 1993), 12–13.

5. Stanley A. Blumberg and Gwinn Owens, *Energy and Conflict: The Life and Times of Edward Teller* (New York: Putnam, 1976), 12, 21.

6. Bertita Harding, *Concerto: The Glowing Story of Clara Schumann* (London: Harrap, 1961), 10, 15.

7. Harvey Sachs, *Rubinstein: A Life in Music* (New York: Grove Press, 1995), 13.

8. M. J. Chorney, "A Quantitative Trait Locus Associated with Cognitive Ability in Children," *Psychological Science* 9, no. 3 (May 1998): 159–166.

9. "U.S. S&E Workforce: Definition, Size, and Growth," National Science Foundation, http://www.nsf.gov/statistics/seind14/index.cfm/chapter-3/c3h.htm#s1.

10. Blumberg and Owens, *Energy and Conflict.*

11. Miles D. Storfer, *Intelligence and Giftedness: The Contribution of Heredity and Early Environment* (San Francisco: Jossey-Bass, 1990), 384–385.

12. Camilla Persson Benbow, "Possible Biological Correlates of Precocious Mathematical Reasoning Ability," *Trends in Neurosciences* 10 (January 1987): 17–20 (especially 18); Lee D. Cranberg and Martin L. Albert, "The Chess Mind," in Loraine K. Obler and Deborah Fein, eds., *The Exceptional Brain: Neuropsychology of Talent and Special Abilities,* (New York: Guilford Press, 1988) (especially 175).

13. Benbow, "Possible Biological Correlates of Precocious Mathematical Reasoning Ability," 59; Storfer, *Intelligence and Giftedness,* 384.

14. Storfer, *Intelligence and Giftedness,* 386, 389.

15. Andrew Hodges, *Alan Turing: The Enigma* (London: Burnett Books, 1983).

16. Ellen Winner, *Gifted Children: Myths and Realities* (New York: Basic Books, 1996), 167.

17. Joan Stiles, "Neural plasticity and cognitive development," *Developmental Neuropsychology* 18, no. 2 (2000): 237–272.

18. Ibid.

19. Roger Highfield and Paul Carter, *The Private Lives of Albert Einstein* (London: Faber and Faber, 1993), 11–12.

20. Weeks, *The Slow Speech Development of a Bright Child,* 63.

21. That might be why some late-talking children begin to speak, not in isolated words, but in phrases or complete sentences. My mother told me that the first thing I said, at age three, was "Go bye-bye in car." Edward Teller began speaking at age four in complete sentences, as have

a number of other late-talking children, including Gary Becker, who grew up to become a Nobel Laureate in economics.

22. "She imitated a number of non-language sounds, such as an airplane overhead, a dog barking, a bird singing, a siren, a fly buzzing, a car starting, or numerous other sounds" (Weeks, *The Slow Speech Development of a Bright Child,* 16).

23. In his autobiography, Rubinstein said that, as a small child, "while nothing would induce me to utter a single word, I was always willing to sing—to imitate with my voice—any sound I heard, thus creating a sensation at home . . . playing the role of a human parrot" (Arthur Rubinstein, *My Young Years* (New York: Knopf, 1973), 4).

24. In Asperger syndrome, there is no significant delay in the onset of speech: "In contrast to Autistic Disorder, there are no clinically significant delays in language" (American Psychiatric Association, *Diagnostic and Statistical Manual of Mental Disorders*, 4th ed. (DSM-IV) (Washington, DC: American Psychiatric Association, 2005), 75).

25. "Nursery school" is the British equivalent of the U.S. term "preschool."

26. Dorothy M. Aram, "Hyperlexia: Reading without Meaning in Young Children." *Topics in Language Disorders* 17, no. 3 (1997): 1–13.

27. Constance Reid, *Julia: A Life in Mathematics* (Washington, DC: Mathematical Association of America, 1996), 5.

24. Denis Brian, *Einstein: A Life* (New York: Wiley, 1996), 3.

25. Blumberg and Owens, *Energy and Conflict.*

26. Sowell, *The Einstein Syndrome,* 47–48.

Chapter 6

1. Tristram Smith, "Discrete Trial Training in the Treatment of Autism." *Focus on Autism and other Developmental Disabilities* 16, no. 2 (2001): 86–92.

2. See Lynn Koegel and Claire LeZebnik, *Overcoming Autism* (New York: Penguin Books, 2005).

3. Jane O'Brien, Tonya Boatwright, Jennifer Chaplin, Charlene Geckler, Doug Gosnell, Jenni Holcombe, and Kelsey Parrish, "The Impact of Positioning Equipment on Play Skills of Physically Impaired Children." *Diversions and Divergences in Fields of Play* 1 (1998): 149.

4. Letter dated November 20, 2007, from Carolyn Stanford Taylor, Assistant State Superintendent, Division for Learning Support, Equity and Advocacy, to Jackson Parker, Interim District Administrator, Racine Unified School District.

5. http://www.gpo.gov/fdsys/pkg/CFR-2010-title42-vol5/pdf/CFR-2010 -title42-vol5-sec482-13.pdf.

6. Rebecca Joan McCauley and Marc E. Fey, eds., *Treatment of Language Disorders in Children*. (Baltimore, MD: Brookes Publishing Company), 2006.

7. Stephen Camarata and Linda Swisher, "A Note on Intelligence Assessment within Studies of Specific Language Impairment," Journal of Speech, Language and Hearing Research 33, no. 1 (1990): 205–207.

8. National Disability Rights Network, 900 Second Street NE, Suite 211, Washington, DC 20002; 02-408-9514; www.ndrn.org.

9. Lawrence D. Shriberg, Dorothy M. Aram, and Joan Kwiatkowski, "Developmental Apraxia of Speech: I. Descriptive and Theoretical Perspectives," *Journal of Speech, Language, and Hearing Research* 40, no. 2 (1997): 273–285.

10. Rebecca J. McCauley, Edythe Strand, Gregory L. Lof, Tracy Schooling, and Tobi Frymark, "Evidence-Based Systematic Review: Effects of Nonspeech Oral Motor Exercises on Speech," *American Journal of Speech-Language Pathology* 18, no. 4 (2009): 343–360.

11. Gregory L. Lof and Maggie M. Watson. "A Nationwide Survey of Nonspeech Oral Motor Exercise Use: Implications for Evidence-Based Practice." *Language, Speech, and Hearing Services in Schools* 39, no. 3 (2008): 392–407.

12. American Academy of Pediatrics, "Sensory Integration Therapies for Children with Developmental and Behavioral Disorders," *Pediatrics* 129, no. 1186. doi: 10.1542/peds.2012-0876.

13. Paul Offit, *Autism's False Prophets: Bad Science, Risky Medicine, and the Search for a Cure*. (New York: Columbia University Press, 2008), 121.

14. Ibid, 123.

15. F. Godlee, J. Smith, and H. Marcovitch, "Wakefield's Article Linking MMR Vaccine and Autism Was Fraudulent," *British Medical Journal* 342 (2012): c17452.

16. Lisa Finestack and Marc Fey, "Evidence Based Intervention for Young Late Talkers," in Late Talkers, ed. Leslie Rescorla and Philip Dale (Baltimore, MD: Brookes Publishing Company), 2013, 283–302.

17. When I began treating children clinically many years ago, I was surprised to receive a phone call from a local pediatrician in Nashville. He said he'd referred three children to me and would be referring more in the future. He explained his reason: I had given three different diagnoses for these children. Only in later years did I learn that many clinicians who evaluate children tend to give the same diagnoses to very different children—a one-size-fits-all approach that can have devastating consequences for a child who doesn't fit their particular preconception.

18. Wendy L. Stone and Theresa Foy DiGeronimo. *Does My Child Have Autism? A Parent's Guide to Early Detection and Intervention in Autism Spectrum Disorders*. Hoboken, NJ: Jossey-Bass, 2006.

Chapter 7

1. For example, see Luigi Girolmetto, Patsy Stieg Pearce, and Elaine Weitzman, "Interactive Focused Stimulation for Toddlers with Expressive Vocabulary Delays," *Journal of Speech & Hearing Research* 39, no. 6 (December 1996): 1274–1282.

2. Girolmetto, Pearce, and Weitzman, "Interactive Focused Stimulation for Toddlers with Expressive Vocabulary Delays"; Janel Sheehan et al.,

"Feasibility of a Language Promotion Program for Toddlers at Risk," *Early Childhood Services: An Interdisciplinary Journal of Effectiveness* 3, no. 1 (March 2009): 33–50.

3. Note that these questions seldom apply to physicians, who are usually examining late-talking children for signs of possible medical conditions that might be delaying their speech development, rather than actually treating the late talking itself, which physicians typically leave to specialists such as speech pathologists.

Chapter 8

1. Robert Owens, *Language Development: An Introduction* (New York: Allyn & Bacon, 2000).

2. Stephen Camarata, "Perspective: Think Developmentally," The ASHA Leader (April 24, 2012), http://www.asha.org/publications/leader/2012/120424/perspective--think-developmentally.htm.

3. Rachel Monahan and Ben Chapman, "Padded 'Calm-Down" Room at Charter School Drives Kids to Anxiety Attacks," New York Daily News, December 11, 2013, http://www.nydailynews.com/new-york/education/padded-calm-down-room-causing-anxiety-kids-article-1.1543983.

Chapter 9

1. Leslie Rescorla, "Age 17 Language and Reading Outcomes in Late-Talking Toddlers: Support for a Dimensional Perspective on Language Delay," *Journal of Speech, Language and Hearing Research* 52, no. 1 (2009): 16–30.

2. Ibid.

3. Janice Rech, Judykay Hartzell, and Larry Stephens, "Comparisons of Mathematical Competencies and Attitudes of Elementary Education Majors with Established Norms of a General College Population," *School Science and Mathematics* 93, no. 3 (1993): 141–144.

4. Anke Buschmann, Bettina Jooss, André Rupp, Friederike Feldhusen, Joachim Pietz, and Heike Philippi, "Parent Based Language Intervention

for 2-Year-Old Children with Specific Expressive Language Delay: A Randomised Controlled Trial," *Archives of Disease in Childhood* 94, no. 2 (2009): 110–116.

5. Winston Churchill, *My Early Life: 1874–1904* (New York, NY: Simon and Schuster), 2010, 13.

6. The books on political thought that my late-talking son and I discussed on that drive home from college included *Leviathan* by Thomas Hobbes and *The Republic* by Plato.

Chapter 10

1. Paul Offit, *Autism's False Prophets: Bad Science, Risky Medicine, and the Search for a Cure* (New York: Columbia University Press, 2008).

2. "Childhood apraxia of speech is a rare severe and persistent speech sound disorder characterized by a deficit in planning/programing oral and laryngeal movements for speech" [emphasis added], quoted in Jennifer J. S. Laffin, Gordana Raca, Craig A. Jackson, Edythe A. Strand, Kathy J. Jakielski, and Lawrence D. Shriberg, "Novel Candidate Genes and Regions for Childhood Apraxia of Speech Identified by Array Comparative Genomic Hybridization," *Genetics in Medicine* 14 (2012): 928–936 (quote on p. 928).

3. After reviewing 45 studies of oral motor exercises to improve speech, Professors Normal Lass and Mary Pannbacker concluded that"the available evidence does not support the continued use of NSOMTs [oral motor exercises such as tongue movements and blowing bubbles or whistles] as a standard treatment and they should be excluded from use as a mainstream treatment until there are further data." Norman J. Lass, and Mary Pannbacker, "The Application of Evidence-Based Practice to Nonspeech Oral Motor Treatments." *Language, Speech, and Hearing Services in Schools* 39.3 (2008): 408–421 (quote on p. 408).

4. The Editors of The Lancet, "Retraction—Ileal-Lymphoid-Nodular Hyperplasia, Non-specific Colitis, and Pervasive Developmental Disorder in Children," *The Lancet* 375, no. 9713 (February 2010): 445.

5. F. Godlee, J. Smith, and H. Marcovitch, "Wakefield's Article Linking MMR Vaccine and Autism Was Fraudulent," *British Medical Journal* 342 (2011): c7452.

6. Michelle Zimmer, Larry Desch, Lawrence D. Rosen, Michelle L. Bailey, David Becker, Timothy P. Culbert, and Hilary McClafferty, et al. "Sensory Integration Therapies for Children with developmental and behavioral disorders." *Pediatrics* 129, no. 6 (2012): 1186–1189.

7. Helen McConachie and Tim Diggle. "Parent Implemented Early Intervention for Young Children with Autism Spectrum Disorder: A Systematic Review," *Journal of Evaluation in Clinical Practice* 13, no. 1 (2007): 120–129; Gerald Mahoney, Ann Kaiser, Luigi Girolametto, James MacDonald, Cordelia Robinson, Philip Safford, and Donna Spiker, "Parent Education in Early Intervention: A Call for a Renewed Focus," *Topics in Early Childhood Special Education* 19, no. 3 (1999): 131140.

Index